D0128056

UNLIMITED
DOUBLES !!

UNLIMITED DOUBLES !!

Finally... a "System" for
out-playing your opponents in tennis.
Anytime. Anywhere.
GUARANTEED.

By Steve Tourdo

Unlimited Doubles and Point Control System
are trademarks of Point Control Technologies

Copyright 2000 By Steve Tourdo. All rights reserved under
International and Pan-American Copyright Conventions.
No part of this book may be reproduced in any form or by any electronic
or mechanical means including information storage and
retrieval systems without permission in writing from
Point Control Technologies, except by a reviewer,
who may quote brief passages in a review.

Published in the United States by
Point Control Technologies
P.O. Box 819 Corte Madera, CA 94976
(800) 631-0673
www.unlimiteddoubles.com

First Paperback Edition 2000   ISBN 0-9676562-0-6

Library of Congress Control Number- 2001118119

Printed and bound in the United States of America.

Edited by Don Clelland
Illustrations by DeGroot Graphics
Cover photo by Colleen Fauteux
Cover design by Edward Cristman

A SPECIAL THANKS to my friends:
Ellen Baker
Dan Campbell
Jim Craig
Colleen Fauteux
Stephen Greffe
Patricia Prince

This book is dedicated in gratitude to all my students
who, in their search for excellence,
have blessed me with the privilege of sharing their journey.

CONTENTS

Introduction

Welcome to *Unlimited Doubles !!* and congratulations for taking the first step toward a better doubles game. You're about to embark on a journey that will forever alter your perception of how doubles is played.

Many tennis players spend years playing the game without really understanding how doubles works. They typically feed the ball into play with a serve or a return and spend the rest of the point reacting to the opponents' shots and hoping for the best... unaware of a better way.

The Point Control System

Unlimited Doubles !! will walk you step-by-step through a "system" that takes the mystery out of building a doubles game. I call it my "Point Control System."

Comprised of eight interrelated building blocks, the Point Control System simplifies and explains the elements of a good doubles game. It dispels the mystery by breaking doubles down to fundamentals that are uncomplicated and flexible enough to be adapted to players' games of all levels. Whether your goal is to move from 3.0 to 4.0 or from 5.0 to 5.5, the Point Control System has what you need. It is a holistic learning system for the self-directed player.

Keep It Simple

Many players feel tennis is the tactical equivalent of chess. In my opinion, it's more like tic-tac-toe... a simple series of moves repeated over and over in a fairly predictable manner where execution makes the difference between winning and losing.

Tactics and Strokes

Tennis is a game of tactics and execution. Before execution can take place, you must have an understanding of tactics. Tactics are the plans to be executed by your strokes and, therefore, come first. This is why *Unlimited Doubles !!* is focused on tactics... because you must have a clear understanding of your tactical wishes before you can expect successful execution of your strokes. To provide a high level of purely tactical instruction, all players are assumed to be of comparable ability and have a complete repertoire of shots. Should there be reference to a shot you're currently lacking, get help from your local pro rather than ignore the tactics.

To Ensure Your Development

•Taking responsibility for your own development is a fundamental principle of learning. Your teaching pro may aid you in your quest, but the power to learn and grow as a player ultimately lies with you.

•Learn to trust in yourself and your ability to distinguish what's right for you. Does the information you're being presented make sense to you? This trust will enable you to distinguish information that's in your best interests for the long haul from a "quick fix" that may be misleading.

•Keep a positive attitude by laughing at your failures and encouraging yourself to learn. If you're to improve, mistakes are inevitable.

•Be patient. Learning to play at a high level is quite challenging. There will be ups and downs in any learning process. Players who follow the lessons and faithfully practice the drills in this book will be rewarded with new levels of tennis skills and understanding.

Doubles is Doubles

Unlimited Doubles !! doesn't differentiate between genders when explaining tactics because tactics have no gender. Tennis ability is not specific to men or women. Hence, the following lessons have no gender specifics and apply equally to men's, women's, and mixed doubles. Efforts to achieve grammatical equality, while well intentioned, frequently lead to awkwardness. To avoid this, *Unlimited Doubles !!* defers to tradition and uses the masculine pronoun throughout.

Using This Book Effectively

Since *Unlimited Doubles !!* builds block upon block; both your understanding and personal improvement will be enhanced if you proceed in the order presented in the book, beginning with lesson one. You'll quickly discover that The Point Control System sometimes uses terms and phrases not common to tennis. Though these terms are explained clearly as the lessons evolve, if you skip around in the book you may miss the explanations.

Each lesson starts with a statement of its objective. This is followed by an easily-understood discussion of what is essential if you are to reach that objective. Next comes a summary of the lesson. Finally, to reinforce your understanding of the role played by that lesson's building block, there is a recommended on-court drill.

These drills form a substructure for *Unlimited Doubles !!,* challenging players to blend concept with practice and muscle memory.

The book is comprised of twelve lessons. The first eight lay the tactical building blocks. Lessons nine through twelve assemble these tactical building blocks of *Unlimited Doubles !!* into a winning strategy. When you understand and can follow these tactics, you'll have a solid understanding of doubles, an understanding you'll be able to use with confidence as you progress from one level to another.

So... enough said. Victory awaits you. Good luck and enjoy.

Lesson 1 - Victory Awaits

How To Ensure You Finish On Top

Objective

Tennis is a competition: as is any game where a score is kept. In such games there are winners and losers. The objective of this lesson is to help you understand that there are only two ways to emerge victorious: (1) you win the match, or (2) the opponents lose the match.

Opponents Trying To Win

Unless the opponents have some reason to believe it impossible, they will begin the match with the objective to BEAT you. All competitive teams want to feel that they have a chance of beating their opponents, so they will come out trying. As your team proves to be too formidable, they will attempt to raise their level of play to out-play you and your partner.

Opponents Hoping You'll Lose

When the opponents feel they can't beat you despite playing their best tennis, their only remaining recourse is to be consistent and hope you LOSE.

For instance: you and your partner are cruising along. You're up 5-2 in the set. Victory is just a matter of time. Suddenly you notice your opponents have changed their style of play. Now they're both hitting the ball more softly and clearing the net by a safe margin. Also, they've moved back toward the baseline. You and your partner find yourselves getting increasingly frustrated. Your opponents aren't "hitting the ball" anymore. Moonballs come drifting lazily toward you. Determined, your team tries harder. Yet the ball keeps coming back. Frustration builds and your errors increase. What happened? Why the reversal in fortunes?

What happened is that your opponents just paid you the ultimate compliment. They decided they couldn't BEAT you, so they asked you to LOSE to them. And you obliged. They simply knocked on a different tennis door and you opened it for them. Remember: your ability and desire to win has to be matched by your ability and desire to AVOID LOSING.

Honesty Pays Off

You are an unusual tennis player if you have never lost a match to a lesser player. And, if you're like most people I've talked to after this type of match, you'll recognize the following:

I approach the player who lost and smile. "What happened?"

"Oh, I just couldn't get it together today, my serve let me down and I kept hitting the tape. Volleys into the net. Just not a good day."

"Would it be fair to say that you gave the match away?"

"No question. Normally, I'd walk all over the guy."

Then I get his opponent aside.

"How'd your match go?"

"Great! I won. I never thought for a moment that I could beat him, but I really played steadily, ran down everything and beat him 6-3."

But from my unbiased viewpoint as a coach, the results are seen in another way. In this hypothetical match, though the lesser player feels he actually won, he'd be on firmer ground if his "win" stemmed from forcing errors and hitting winners, rather than from depending on points he got from his opponent's unforced errors, points lost for no tactical reason. The lesson here is that you must make and accept, for the sake of your growth as a player, the honest distinction between matches where you won and matches where your opponents lost. To do otherwise is to slow your development.

Beating Your Opponents

Beating your opponents begins with the intention to do so and then you develop the means. To truly "beat" your opponents you must force errors. It may seem obvious, but that's what the Point Control System is teaching you... how to beat opponents you weren't able to beat before. Paradoxically, to truly grasp this concept you need to know its opposite as well.

"Please Lose to Us"

The tactical opposite to beating your opponents is to ask them to lose. For right now, know that you do this by taking less risk. To ask the opponents to lose to you, you must be more consistent than they are. You know they're losing when they make unforced errors.

When you take less risk, instead of attacking, it often frustrates and wreaks emotional havoc with opponents who haven't yet learned to handle changing roles. Their egos begin to overcome reason. They can't believe a player like you (perceived "junker") is even on the same court with them. They begin to lose points, then they begin to lose control. Angry with themselves, they try harder and sink faster. Fortunately for you, they haven't stopped to realize that your team is just hanging on by a thread; if they won't lose to you there's nothing else you can do.

Giving Yourself Options

Although you cannot simultaneously play to beat your opponents and ask them to lose to you, you can and should learn to use both approaches. Then, assess and make the choice that's appropriate. Most teams that get blind-sided by the "please lose to me" tactic never use this tactic themselves. Once you're familiar with this option and able to recognize it, you shouldn't lose to opponents using it against you. If you're out-playing them, expect them to test your consistency and patience. It's all they have left if your other tactics are trouncing them.

Recognition that change has occurred is critical to your response. Therefore: PAY ATTENTION! Watch for a change in tactics when you're winning handily. Against a smart team, you should expect this. It's just a matter of time until they check to see if you'll lose to them. At the pre-4.0 level the change is usually obvious. Maybe the opponents will huddle and converse and when they resume play the net man has joined his partner on the baseline and the lobbing begins. Above 4.0, however, the transition is less obvious and the superior skills of the players permit them to refine the change. They reduce their risk by starting to clear the net by an additional foot or so, and are more conservative on important points. Still, although more difficult to detect, the change in tactics reflects a change in attitude. It is important that you recognize the route your opponents are now taking to claim victory in order to respond effectively.

Note: there will be times when even the strongest players will need to slow down overwhelming opponents. This is being smart, not wimpy.

To Summarize

There are two ways to emerge the victor in a tennis match: beat the opponents by forcing errors, or let them lose to you through unforced errors. Determine which means your opponents are using against you. Then decide upon a tactic. If you're far ahead in the match, expect your opponents to test your complacency and, maybe, your flexibility. They'll ask you to lose to them. Smile. It's both their last resort and the ultimate compliment.

Point Control System Drill

This drill requires four players. It is one of the most valuable you'll ever work on. In fact, it is the foundation of tactics. The drill begins with two players on each baseline. One team is the now-familiar "please lose to me" team. The other is the aggressive team. Games are played to five points. Each begins with the "lose to me" team feeding the ball as a groundstroke to one of the aggressors. The feeding team's objective is to keep the ball in play, returning it steadily, avoiding errors that give away points. Regardless of the court position necessary to stay in the rally, their intention is to be consistent and not "lose" any points. The aggressive team should try to break through this tactic by attacking to win the points. Done this way, the drill results in one side trying to beat its opponents, while the other "asks them to lose." By rotating positions each player will get an opportunity to switch roles.

Congratulations!

You've completed the first building block. Proceed to the next lesson.

Lesson 2 - Consistency
How To Build A Consistent Game

Objective

Consistency is one of the most important traits of a solid doubles game. In this lesson, you'll learn how to improve your consistency in order to avoid falling victim to the opponent's "please-lose-to-me" style through unforced errors.

What Is Consistency?

Within the Point Control System, we define consistency as: "the ability to repeatedly hit your chosen target." Ironically, the start point for incorporating this critical element into your game, choosing a target, is the element most often ignored.

Targets Lead To Accuracy

If we are doing a drill and a student errs and wonders what he did wrong, I always ask, "Where were you aiming?"

He may stop and think for a moment, then reply sheepishly, "Well, I wasn't really aiming."

I shrug, "Then you didn't really miss."

Sometimes he'll look disappointed at my reply. He probably expected me to say "You didn't bend your knees enough, or you took your eye off the ball." But slowly the truth begins to sink in and he realizes that before I can tell him why or how he missed the target, he has to have chosen one and tried to hit it.

If you don't choose a target, you deprive yourself of the "starter" that sets in motion the vital parts of stroke production and tactics. Choosing targets and stroking toward them will lead to accuracy. Accuracy then opens the door to consistency.

The Target Factor

The first factor is understanding how to choose targets. As a general rule, the smaller the target you choose, the less consistent you'll be in hitting it. The larger the target you're able to choose, the greater your chances of hitting it.

Choose targets that are appropriate for your level. For a 3.0 player returning serve, a target such as "crosscourt" might be adequate tactically and lend itself well to consistency. However, for a 4.5 player, "crosscourt" is not tactically damaging enough. He needs a more specific target like "low and in the server's alley." If he struggles to be consistent with this target, he might lower his target expectations to just "crosscourt and over the net" until the required consistency returns and then aim again at the original target. The difficulty level of the target you choose dictates how difficult or easy it will be to be consistent.

Even the top pros double-fault, but it's seldom because they can't get their second serve into that big service box. They could do that all day. However, when their opponent's return is so strong that the second serve has to be placed in a very small area in the corner of the box, double-faults increase. And, just as the pros do, you have to select your targets according to the opponents you're playing, always keeping in mind that larger targets lend themselves better to consistency than do smaller ones.

The Net Clearance Factor

You've all seen those players who clear the net by five feet, hit nothing but moonballs, and never seem to miss. Clearing the net by a greater margin is an excellent way to drive up your consistency level, especially if you're in the habit of over-hitting or hitting the net.

Your opponents will determine your allowable net clearance by the quality of their net games. Unless the opponents are all over the net, allow yourself some clearance. Nothing makes less sense than hitting the net tape when the opponent is camped on the baseline.

The Power Factor

The third factor in consistency is power. Players who try to hit a winner on every shot will naturally struggle to be consistent. These players attempt to ruin the consistency of the opponents by subjecting them to unmanageable levels of power. However, the harder they hit the ball, the lower their own level of consistency. Much like an automobile that's driven too fast for a curvy road, too much power diminishes control.

The Stroke Mechanics Factor

"Moonballers," on the other hand, are at the opposite end of the spectrum. They rarely miss because they hit the ball so softly that they can do this with very simple stroke mechanics.

The purpose of this book is not to teach you the stroke mechanics. However, I will say that stroke mechanics have a direct relationship to consistency. Some strokes are very long and swingy. These strokes don't lend themselves to consistency because their mechanics contain too much timing risk.

One player who comes to mind as really understanding this concept is John McEnroe. Mr. McEnroe is probably the greatest doubles player of all time. In fact, it has been said that the greatest doubles team in the world is John McEnroe and anyone else! He uses stroke mechanics that could have been designed by a physics professor. His backhand return of serve, for example, is a work of simple artistry compared to many of his counterparts. Consequently, it produces a high level of consistency while generating efficient, manageable power. (To incorporate this same understanding into your own game, use short backswings on ground strokes, minimal spin, and take out any swing in your volleys.)

The Time Factor

Proper use of time also can help your consistency. In addition to shortening your strokes, another way to create the feeling of having more time is to vary the timing of your split-step. This will be discussed in detail in Lesson 5. For now, know that the usual time to split-step is when the opponent is about to strike the ball. If you find you need more time, split-step earlier. The timing of the split-step is something you can adjust to suit your need for time... and time affects consistency.

How Many In A Row Is "Consistent"?

No matter how hard you hit it, you can't become a successful tennis player with one shot in a row. If you intend to play at a level where your opponents can sustain even a short rally, you'll need a few shots in succession. Set your sights on three. With three shots in a row your team can sustain a six shot exchange. If you've ever counted the number of hits in your doubles points you'll realize a six-shot exchange is quite long. Assume you are adequately consistent if you can make three shots in a row. Later we'll learn more on how the three shots link together to become the backbone for creating a tactical plan to beat the opponents.

Frame Of Mind Plays A Role

A large component of consistency is mental. <u>The Inner Game of Tennis</u> by W. Timothy Gallwey is an excellent book on how thought processes interact with kinesthetics and I would not do him justice by attempting to paraphrase his ideas here. However, I will suggest that internal consistency leads to external consistency. Think of yourself as a solid, consistent player and expect the ball to come back. That's what it means to play a worthy opponent. Expecting the ball to come back is a basic component of consistency because without that assumption you have no need for consistency. You'll know you're truly achieving consistency when you feel a little disappointed the opponent didn't get the ball back one more time!

Balance

Maintaining balance is an important function of the body. Without it, ordinary functions like walking and bending over would be difficult, at best. Complex physical activities like playing tennis would be completely impossible. Your body has an innate ability to maintain its balance, provided you don't overtax it. As a biological priority, your body will try to regain lost balance to the detriment of other, less necessary functions, such as hitting a tennis ball. It is essential that you consciously try to conserve your balance when entering and exiting shots, split-stepping, etc. If you are off-balance, your body's natural priority system will override unnecessary activities (playing tennis, for example) to concentrate on the essential function of returning to a balanced state. If you stay balanced in the first place, you have more of your body's natural physical abilities left to devote to hitting a tennis ball. We've already mentioned the importance of consistency in your play. Consistency is impossible unless you maintain your balance. Enter and exit all shots with your balance in-tact. If you have to struggle to maintain balance, don't hit so hard. You only have the right to use as much power as you can control with your balance intact.

Three Examples Of The "Consistency Game"

It's deuce at 4-4 in the third set and you have the privilege of returning serve for this important point. You know the server has a solid first volley, but also know he'll be feeling the pressure of the moment. Normally, you'd rip the return to the server's feet, but you feel a little more consistency is in order. In this situation, clear the net with more margin than usual. This introduces a little bit of "please lose to me" in the shot and gives the server the opportunity to miss if he's so inclined. Shorten your backswing to eliminate unnecessary timing risk and use a nice smooth follow through.

It's windy and sunny out and you are the lucky recipient of a sky-high lob that's right in the sun. Normally you'd go for an angle off the court, but you feel a little more consistency is in order. Choose the middle of the court at about the service line as the target for your overhead. Cut the power bit and abbreviate the stroke. Your opponents are at the baseline anyway, so the best they could do is lob again and maybe the next will be easier to handle.

The opposing net player has been poaching like crazy on his partner's serve, making it difficult for you to be consistent with your return. You know he needs to be kept honest and you're tempted to blast one down the line, but you feel a little more consistency is in order. For consistency, use the lob rather than blasting the return down the line. It gives you more margin for error by requiring less pace, allowing for simpler mechanics, and allows you to play a damaging shot without aiming near the lines.

To Summarize

To win a point, you need be only one shot more consistent than your opponent. Select the factors in your "consistency game" that meet the tactical needs of the moment. From your arsenal decide what serves you best: choosing larger targets, increasing net clearance, cutting pace, simplifying your strokes or split-stepping earlier.

Point Control System Drill

For this drill you will need a partner. The idea is to play on half a doubles court including the alleys. Deuce to deuce and ad to ad. One player serves and the other returns. The object is to hit three shots per side. Be nice to each other and help extend the point to a six shot rally. You may serve and volley just as in a real point. If you're someone who stays back, then do that and make your three shots in a row without missing.

Once you can regularly accomplish this, you may be a little more aggressive about winning the point. Practice using the factors of the "consistency game" to reach three hits per side. Rotate the serve and the sides of the court until all are experienced.

Congratulations!

You have completed the lesson on consistency. You are now ready to build on this knowledge by moving to the next lesson.

Lesson 3 - Where Am I?

How To Master Court Positioning

Objective

Court positioning is the basis for controlling the opponents. Because, while the opponents ultimately choose the shot they will hit, their selection is based on your court position. To be in control, you'll need to have a clear understanding of exactly where you are on the court and how your (and your partner's) position affects the opponents.

In this lesson, you will learn where to be on the court when your opponent is hitting the ball.

Progress Based On Two Assumptions

You need to understand court positioning if you're going to be able to reach your opponents' shots. Obviously, if they were willing to hit every ball directly to you, you wouldn't need to worry about your position. However, as you know, they are seldom that cooperative.

To appreciate the value of this building block, we'll have to make two assumptions about your opponents: (1) they are on the court to beat you with their shot-making, not to rely on your unforced errors, and (2) given a choice, they would rather hit the ball away from you than to you or at you.

Players And Space

When a doubles team comes to the net, the bodies of its players physically obstruct two areas of the court. The rest of the space is open. Opponents can use this open space by hitting between the players at the net, or going for the left or right alleys. The net players may also be avoided by going over them. To simplify: there are five openings on the court, three for passing shots and two for lobs. (Diagram #1)

Being "Neutral" To The Opponents

When you and your partner take "neutral" court positions, you are in the middle of all available shots from the opponents. Therefore, your court positions are not inviting any particular incoming shot. Knowing a "neutral" court position is as vital to tactics as a ready position is to stroke production. It's the salesperson-equivalent of "How can I help you?" It allows you to observe your opponents and recognize their tactical tendencies.

In later lessons we'll work toward more advanced skills, such as anticipation and poaching. For now, however, let's restrict our efforts to constructing a base that shows you how to be "neutrally in-position" to your opponents.

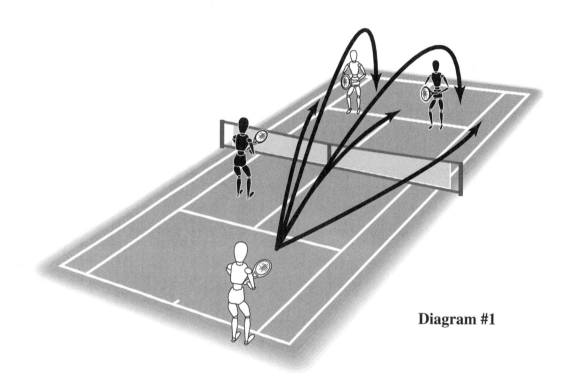

Diagram #1

You can avoid players by hitting to the left alley,
right alley, between them, or over them.
Five openings (3 passing shots and 2 lobs).

   Lesson 3 - Where Am I?

The Left / Right Dimension

Passing shots are conclusive. They instantly end the point. If you make a major mistake in your left/right positioning, you expose your team to these decisive shots. Assume, when your opponents line up opposite you on the court, that they see two players and three openings in the left/right dimension. You, to thwart whatever plans your opponents may have, must make sure you and your partner are "in position," that is, in the area of the court that marks the middle of the potential action. But, beware, for "middle" can be a deceptive word.

To find your team's middle you need to know two things: (1) from where is the incoming ball being hit? In other words, where is the hitter on his court? (2) how much of your court is actually available to him? That figured out, you should position your team in the middle of this "available" court. By positioning yourselves in this manner, you keep constant the size of the openings at the net. By keeping them the same size, you send your opponents what I call a "neutral" right/left message. To make this clear, let's use a few examples.

First, place the hitting opponent (who, by the way, is the only opponent who matters at this point), in the center of his court. If he hits to the right of your team, his best shot could land on the doubles sideline at the same depth as the service line. His best shot to the left of your team could land in the same spot on the left sideline. These two are not only the best possible shots to your team's outside, they are the best shots physically possible. (Diagram #2)

Without meaning to sound like a geometry teacher, if we shaded the area between these two possible shots from your opponent, they would form a triangle (apex at the opponent). This represents the opponent's potential angle of return. (Diagram #3)

To be "in position" you merely bisect (divide into equal parts) this potential angle of return. For singles this line would run through the center of the court. For doubles the line would run through the center of each half of the court. Therefore, you need to be somewhere on this bisecting line. Since we've chosen net positions for our example, if you and your partner centered yourselves in the service boxes, you would be "in position" for a shot coming from the middle of the opponent's court. (Diagram #4)

Notice that the potential angle of return, as illustrated, does not cover the entire playing surface. To hit the court surface outside the shaded areas would require extreme

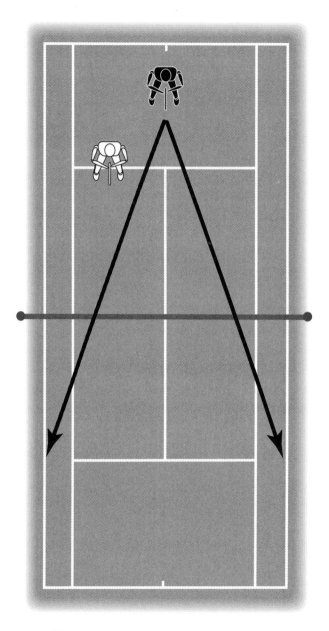

These two lines represent the best shots possible
to either side of your team by an opponent
who is in the center of the court.

Diagram #2

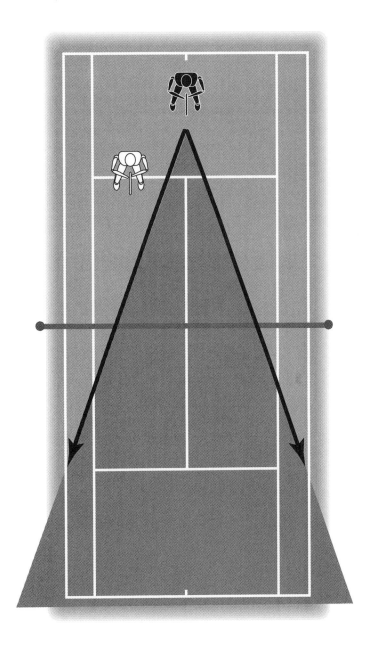

Potential Angle of Return

Diagram #3

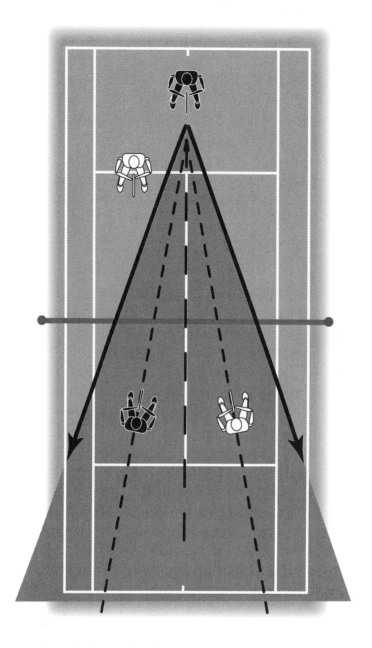

Neutrally "in-position" for a shot coming from the center.

Diagram #4

accuracy with low velocity. Drop shots are the only shots that would have access to this court area, and they can be reached easily when you're at the net.

Here's another example to help clarify the concept of court positioning. This time your opponent is hitting the ball from the deuce court alley. His best possible shot to the right of your team would land on the sideline at service-line depth. His best possible shot to your left would duplicate this, only to your left. These two shots constitute the potential angle of return for an opponent hitting from the deuce court alley. This time your team has to re-position itself slightly to the left. For simplicity, let's consider the best spot to be half way between the middle of the service box and the left sideline of the service box. Should the hitting opponent start from the ad court alley, your response would be a mirror image of the foregoing. (Diagram #5)

Front / Rear Dimension

Making a major mistake in left/right dimension exposes your team to passing shots. Making a mistake in the front/rear dimension will either get you lobbed, if you're too close to the net, or allow your opponents to hit at your feet, which will force you to hit up if you're too far from the net.

To send a neutral message concerning your front/rear positioning you need to stand where you're just as apt to be lobbed as to have your feet hit.

"Neutral" is one-third of the distance from the service line to the net. Deeper than this, you will be discouraging lobs, but encouraging your opponents to hit low at your feet. Closer than the one-third "Neutral Net," you make your feet less of a target, but you encourage your opponents to lob. (Diagram #6)

To Summarize

There are two dimensions to the court, left/right and front/rear. You and your partner will be in a neutral position if you are in the center of the potential angle of return for the left/right dimension, and at the one-third mark for the front/rear.

Point Control System Drill

You and your partner are to help each other solidify the feeling of what it means to be "in-position." One of you is to move around the court to various positions as a make-believe opponent who is about to hit the ball. The other player will move around the

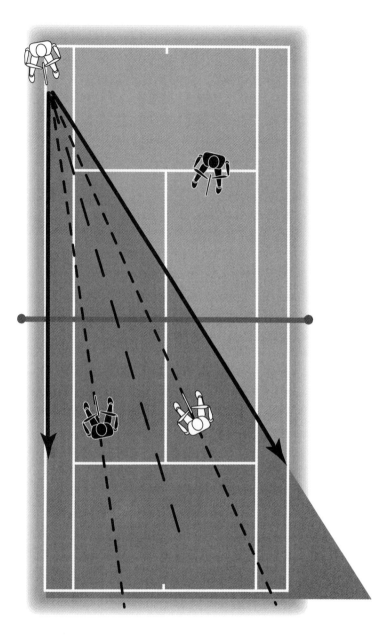

When the hitting opponent changes position,
the angle of return changes.

Diagram #5

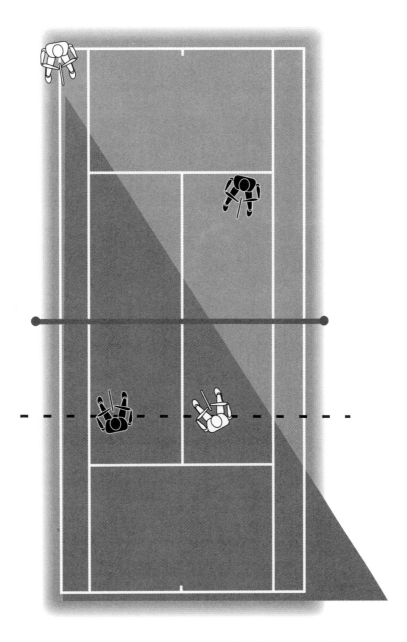

One-third of the way from the service line to the net is
considered "neutral" in the front / rear dimension.

Diagram #6

1/3 mark on the other side of the court attempting to stay "in position" no matter where the other player moves. He should practice as both an ad and deuce court player.

Start by using the positions from the examples and then make up new ones. Notice how the hitter moves much more than the net player who's staying in-position at the net.

After you try several different hitting positions by roaming around the court, switch roles and let your partner try.

Congratulations!

You've completed what you need to know for the present about court positioning. We will, however, return to the subject later to point out some important distinctions. Now you're ready to move on to the next lesson.

Lesson 4 - Don't Be Nice

How To Hit Away From Your Opponents

The Objective

Ask almost any player if he'd rather hit to his opponents or avoid them and the answer is obvious. Despite this, however, many of these same players struggle to incorporate this tactic into their games. While they grasp it intellectually, on the court they don't do it. The objective in this lesson is to teach you how to focus on the openings rather than on your opponents.

You Hit What You Focus On

In a lifetime of reading, you've subconsciously learned to focus on black letters against a white background. In the rearrangement above, we've reversed the letters and the background, forcing you to make an adjustment. To read the words, you've changed to focus on white letters against a black background. The objective of this lesson is similar to that change. See your opponents as frames for the openings you're trying to hit. Learn to focus on the openings, rather than the players. You must shift your perspective and concentrate on the three holes in the right/left dimension and the two lobs. Work on it and you'll change. It's not difficult; just different.

Experience Talks

I'll never forget an extremely valuable lesson I received when I started learning to hang glide. After several flights off the "bunny hill," I was about to make my first flight of any real altitude. The landing zone itself was a large open field with few obstacles, not a difficult target to hit, particularly since the early flights began in the landing zone and only carried about seventy-five feet.

But, for this flight, I was launched from a one-hundred foot hill, farther from the landing zone. My instructor gave me explicit instructions on what to do, and what to focus on. He stressed the importance of concentrating; zeroing-in on the area where I wanted to land. Almost as soon as I got airborne, it hit me that looking down from a hundred feet was quite a bit different from skimming along at ten feet. My flight plan was to head straight toward the landing zone, turn right over the large trees and come upwind for a landing.

Well, as I crossed the edge of the landing zone, I unconsciously began to focus on the trees beyond. I'd never noticed them before. They seemed awfully close to the spot I'd picked for my landing. Suddenly, they got closer and closer and I could hear my instructor yelling. His voice sounded like it was coming from the trees. Fortunately, I snapped out of my fixation on them in time to zoom overhead by about five feet. Somehow, my focus then swerved back to the landing zone and I came in for a very nervous touchdown. I was wiping the sweat away as my instructor sprinted up. When he caught his breath, he gave me this invaluable advice: "Steve, always focus on the spot where you want to land; focus on it and you'll hit it."

The Advantages

There are three advantages to hitting the openings: (1) you force your opponents to move, (2) you create an opening for your following shot, (3) you become more aware that the opponents will be aiming at *your* openings when the situation is reversed.

Forcing Motion

When you hit an opening, you force your opponents to move, or lose the point. Regardless, many players simply won't move. It's not because they're slow or lazy that they remain anchored. People they've played have conditioned them, by hitting balls directly to their racquets (often by accident), that there is tennis profit in standing still.

While you also may often be able to hit directly to your opponents and rely on their errors, I strongly suggest you abandon this approach and begin to hit the openings instead. You should keep in mind one of the primary building blocks of tactics: it is better to hit away from an opponent than toward him. After all, if he sometimes misses when you lay the ball on his racquet, imagine what it will be like when you make him move!

When you shift from hitting toward your opponents to hitting away from them, you make a major tactical advance toward the next-higher level of play. Hits directed toward the openings continue to get points from opponents who refuse to move. Furthermore, by your shift in approach, you require them to play at a level they're not familiar with. This new level requires your opponents to have anticipatory skills, split-steps, and the ability to process information more quickly (skills *you* will learn as the lessons progress).

When your opponents do move toward the ball, they confront new problems. Balance, accuracy and power are all adversely affected by having to change court position. Simply put, almost everyone hits the ball better when it's directed toward, rather than away from, him.

Open The Court

Hitting to an opening is the best way to create an opening for your next shot. One characteristic of the 4.0-and-above player is increased consistency. Players of these levels will be anticipating the possibility of a "next shot," because there often is one. Therefore, opening the court *for* the next shot is important. If the opponent doesn't get back "in position" before you strike the ball, you will have an open court to hit to.

Getting What You Give

Players who hit the openings will assume their opponents will do the same. This assumption then becomes a foundation that facilitates anticipation. Wouldn't it be helpful to have advance warning as to which opening your opponents plan to use? In Lesson 8, you will learn that skill. However, for right now, I'd like to point out one more detail about hitting the openings that will make your shots even more effective: hit the ball through the opening so that it strikes the court at the same distance from the net as the opponent's stance. For example, if he is at a neutral front/rear position (one-third of the distance to the net from the service line), hit the ball so it lands at the one-third point. This bounce-point ensures a difficult play for the opponent, even if he anticipates which opening you've chosen. (Diagram #7)

To Summarize

Learn to focus on the openings rather than the players. The players are only there to define the openings. When hitting an opening, choose a bounce-point at the same depth as your opponent's feet. This will avoid giving him an easy shot at a routine ball.

Point Control System Drill

You will need a partner for this drill. Place two chairs, or even gear bags, at the one-third mark in the center of the service boxes to simulate opponents. You and your partner take positions that mirror these markers on the opposite side of the net. Shift your perspective to see the openings not the markers. Now focus on the markers.

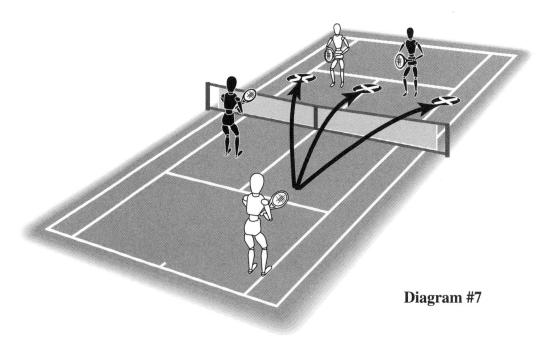

Diagram #7

To increase the effectiveness of your shots
to the openings, use a bounce-point that is the
same depth as your opponents are positioned.

Shift back to seeing the openings. Do this several times until you can feel the different perspectives when focusing on the openings.

One of you go to the "opponent's" side of the net and feed balls to the net player who will practice hitting volleys into all of the openings. Rotate positions as feeder and hitter. Try different court positions as well.

Place the hitter in the alley for example, and place the chairs in proper bisection as though they were actual opponents who know what they're doing. Begin again and practice volleying to the openings.

Congratulations!

You've completed the lesson on the importance of focusing on and hitting to the openings. You are now ready to build on this knowledge by moving to the next lesson.

Lesson 5 - Moving With The Flow

How To Ensure Fluid Movement

Objective

Flowing smoothly on the court is a common characteristic of anyone who plays tennis well. In this lesson you'll learn to move in harmony with the coming and going action of a multi-hit rally. This is a very easy lesson to comprehend intellectually and with some practice of the Point Control System Drill, you will quickly incorporate this fluidity into your game.

The "Flow"

Breath moves in and out of your body in a manner much like the flow of action during a point. When you breathe, you exhale, pause and inhale. In the flow of court action, there is an outgoing flow, a change in direction, and an incoming flow. A ball in play is either moving away from your team toward its target, being struck by an opponent, or moving back toward you. This three component cycle continues to repeat itself until the point is over.

The "In-Position Closure"

Let's say you've just served the ball and it's on its way to the receiver. You've decided that you would rather be closer to the net than stay at the baseline. The time to move to your desired court position is when the ball is moving toward the receiver. Within the Point Control System, this movement toward a more desirable position when the ball is moving away is called the "in-position closure."

Use the ball's "away" time to take the court position you feel appropriate, considering where your ball is heading. If you've earned the right to move forward, the "in-position closure" could be a forward motion. Or, if you've hit a short lob and need more reaction time, the "in-position closure" could be a backward movement. You also use it to go right or left into bisection for the particular angle of return.

Timing for "in-position closure" begins when you strike the ball and ends when the ball is about to be struck by your opponent. If you stay in flow with the action on the court you can probably move comfortably within this time-frame. But if you disrupt the flow by exceeding the time allowed, for example, by continuing forward while the opponent is hitting the ball, your discomfort level will rise. If he hits the ball right back to you, you may get away with it. However, think about it: don't the players you aspire to play against hit toward the openings? (Diagram #8)

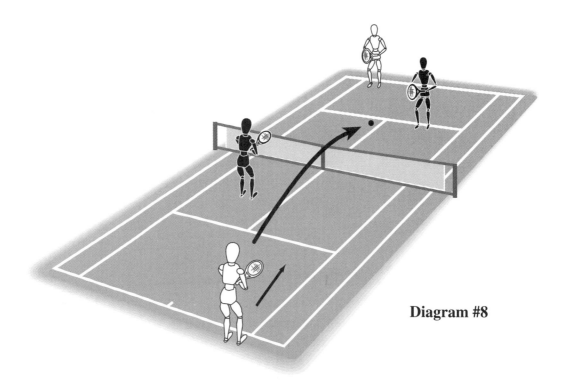

Diagram #8

Change your court position
while the ball is moving AWAY from your team.

Should you find there isn't enough time to reach your desired court position prior to your shot arriving at the opponent, you may be hitting too hard. The idea is to get to your desired court position at or before the opponent is able to play the ball. If this is not happening, correct it in one of two ways: (1) hit your outgoing ball with less pace to give yourself time to get into position, or (2) move more quickly!

The "Split-Step"

Just before the opponent is to strike the ball you do what is commonly called a "split-step." This is a MOMENTARY placing of both feet simultaneously, shoulder width apart. Your knees should be bent to enable you to push off in any direction necessary. Your racket is held in the ready position. The idea of split-stepping is like going into an unfamiliar corner while driving a car: you tap the brakes to reduce speed as a precaution in case you need to make a major directional change. Then, step on the gas again as you proceed through the corner. (Diagram #9)

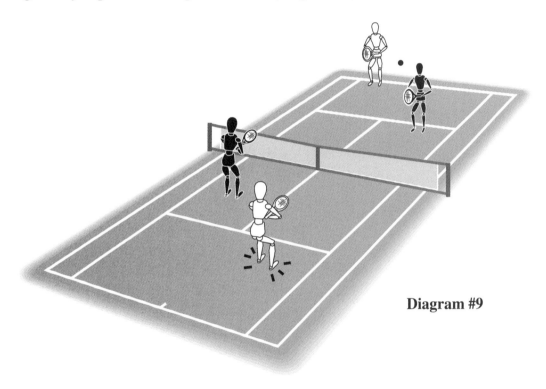

Diagram #9

"Split-Step" when the ball is about to be hit by the opponent.

It's important to note that this is not a complete stop. Just a momentary pause recognizing your opponent's ability to require you to change direction (*if* they're aiming for the openings!). A split-step provides you with the required balance-base from which to meet his challenge. This stability also provides you with more response time and adds to your composure. And, as you'll quickly discover, composure is of much more value than an extra forward step of "in-position closure."

The exact split-step timing is ultimately up to you. You have to determine what you need in order to make directional changes. However, as a simple guideline, I suggest the split-step be done just *before* your opponent strikes the ball. If he's unpredictable, your game is a little off, you're nervous or feeling overpowered, adjust. Split-step a little earlier. Take your time and opt for quality. EXECUTING A CONTROLLED SHOT FROM DEEPER IN THE COURT IS PREFERABLE TO A RUSHED AND POORLY EXECUTED SHOT FROM CLOSER TO THE NET.

Keep in mind that your court position when you split-step defines both where you are and where the openings in your court are. Your awareness of the latter and your knowledge of the effect your court position has on your opponents' shot selections are important components to anticipation, which will be covered in Lesson 8.

Once you've split-stepped and seen the incoming ball, you simply "hit the gas" again and move to the ball.

The "To-The-Ball Closure"

The ball is now on the way back toward your team (headed for one of the openings on your side of the net) and you're on the move again, only this time you're headed for the ball with the intention of returning it to your chosen target.

This "to-the-ball" movement could be one step or many and should be made in whatever direction is necessary to intercept the ball. Keep in mind, however, that closures toward the net are better for your team than closures away from the net. Think Forward. If that's not possible, improvise and get to the ball. (Diagram #10)

The Next Verse

Once you or your partner hits the ball, the process begins all over again with your team's movement to get "in position" as the ball moves toward its target. This is followed by a "split-step" as the ball nears the hitting opponent, and then your "to-the-ball closure." This cycle continues until the point is over.

Common Challenges

The most common problem I find with players who don't flow smoothly on the court is that either they don't split-step or, they "split-STOP" (don't move forward again when the ball is coming toward them). Practicing this lesson's Point Control System Drill will cure these problems.

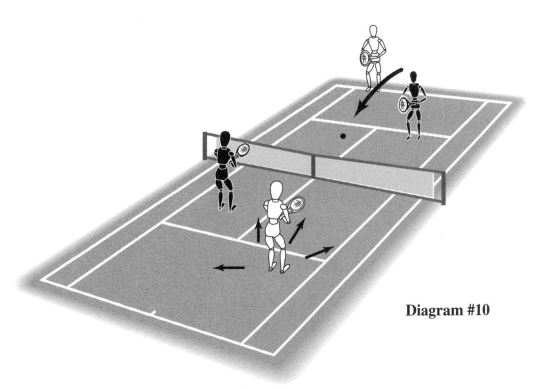

Diagram #10

When the ball is moving toward your team,
move to the ball. This "to-the-ball closure" is best
done forward unless the opponents have lobbed.

To Summarize

When the ball is moving away from your team, you're moving to a more desirable version of "in-position." An instant before your opponent hits, you split-step to ensure a balance point from which you can change direction. When the ball is moving towards your team, you're moving to the ball the opponents have hit toward their chosen target. Keep this timing in mind and you'll flow smoothly with the action.

Point Control System Drill

This is a two-player drill. One player serves nicely to his partner who is the receiver. The receiver hits the return crosscourt right *to* the server, and is done- he doesn't hit any more balls. The object is for the server to work on his in-position closure, split-step, and to-the-ball closure in a low pressure environment where only the first volley is played. Do not play the point out, just practice serving, moving forward, split-stepping as the opponent is about to hit, and then moving forward to get ONE volley.

If it helps, put markers on the court to represent the spot where you intend doing your split-step. Then, pay attention to whether you volleyed from this same spot (ball hits you) or if you used your to-the-ball closure to advance forward (you hit ball). Don't worry about how far you make your way into the court during your in-position closure. Split-step at a distance that's comfortable for you given your foot speed and the speed of your serve.

Do ten each until you begin to feel yourself smoothly flowing through these two hits, then reverse the drill to let your partner serve and volley while you return.

Congratulations!

You have now completed the lesson on flowing smoothly on the court, and are ready to build on this knowledge by moving to the next lesson.

Lesson 6 - The Three Zones

How To Stay On Schedule To Win

Objective

In the lesson on consistency you learned that three shots in a row, as a team, is considered "consistent" in most doubles arenas. Three shots can be enough if you understand how to use them. The objective of this lesson is to teach you how to stay on schedule to win in three shots.

"Eat" Your Way To The Point

A chef preparing dinner knows he has roughly three courses to satisfy the appetite of his customer. He plans to serve an appetizer, entree, and dessert. By the end of the meal he wants the customer to have had enough food. Hence, he is on a three course schedule to satisfaction.

"Tactical 10"

On the tennis court, instead of satisfying your customer, you're beating your opponents. Like the chef, you have three courses (shots) with which to accomplish this feat. A "tactical 10" (abbreviated to T10) means your opponents have had enough... the point is over. Perhaps because you've beaten them with your three shots or perhaps because they've lost the point on an unforced error. The fact is, you have opponents who have had enough.

The "Three Zone Concept"

There are three basic types of tactical shots within the Point Control System and they're hit from the "zones" of the court that bear their names. If you are to be consistent and do severe tactical damage to the opponents in three shots, it is very important to have a strong grasp of these three types of shots. I call them "entrance" shots, "transition" shots, and "net" shots. To beat your opponents on a three-shot schedule requires that you plan to hit one shot from each of these zones. (Diagram #11)

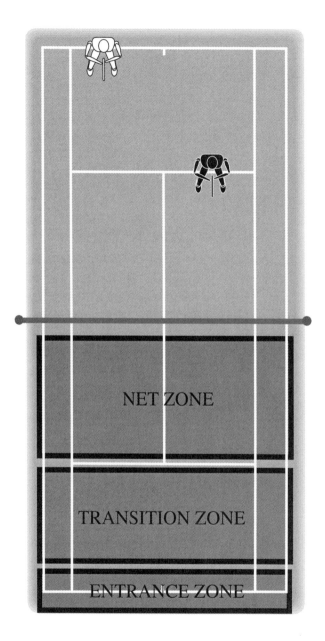

NET ZONE

TRANSITION ZONE

ENTRANCE ZONE

Think of the court as being comprised of three zones.
To win in three shots... hit one from each zone.

Diagram #11

Entrance Zone

Entrance shots are used to enter the point. They are your first exposure to the ball and are as important to tennis as making a good first impression in a job interview. If you begin on a poor note, it's difficult (though not impossible) to recover.

The entrance shots are hit from the entrance zone at or near the baseline. These are generally serves and service returns. Entering the point with a strong tactical number will require less work with your team's next two shots. However, it is not the place to be attempting to hit "T10s." This will wreak havoc with your consistency and is not necessary if you hit three shots in a row. Attempting a "T10" entrance shot can be compared to trying to land a job with the handshake on the initial interview; it happens, but rarely. Rather, make a strong first impression and use the next two interviews to get the job.

Enter the point motivated by a solid tactical intention like serving down the middle or returning at the server's feet. Keep in mind that you have two additional shots to finish your opponents off. If all goes well, you'll only have to make one shot from the entrance zone, because once you've entered the point with either your serve or your return, you'll be moving forward (in-position closure) through the "transition zone."

Transition Zone

Transition shots are played from the area between the baseline and the service line. This is called the "transition zone" because you must pass through it as you move from the entrance zone to the net zone. Normally, you should have to hit only a single transition shot. Although this zone is not a place to hang out, it's not a place to be feared, either.

Names like "no man's land" for the transition zone give shots hit from this area an ominous undertone. But there actually is no such place, since all players on the way to the net must pass through this zone. Nevertheless, to feel comfortable in "no-man's land," hone your half-volley skills, because you're probably going to have to handle balls hit to your feet. If you don't have a reliable half-volley, get some help and learn one. You cannot advance to the higher levels without this shot. Players who do not have a half-volley and consequently sprint to the net to avoid "no-man's land," set themselves up for another problem: the lob over their partner's head. Confronted with this, the server will most likely slow his approach to the net, making himself vulnerable to shots hit to his feet in the transition zone.

A well-placed transition shot can pave the way for an easy volley in the net zone. There are only two criteria for a successful transition. First, and most important, keep the ball low if you want to move forward to the net zone. Advancing behind a high ball can be very challenging and make for an extremely difficult (if not painful!) shot. Second, try to hit an opening. When you've built up your competence, challenge yourself, hit low *and* into an opening. If you can do this consistently, you have a world-class transition and should have an open court for your next volley.

Obviously, a transition shot is only a transition shot if you actually transition. If you have to hit a second or third shot from that area, you didn't transition, but you did reduce your chances to win the point. When you've earned the right to get to the net by hitting a low transition shot, you'll want to go forward. Keep the ball low, continue in and finish them off from the net zone.

Net Zone

The net zone is the area between the service line and the net. This is where consistent players trying to beat their opponents will complete their three-shot flurry of tactical devastation. Generally, the net zone shot will be the third in your three-shot series. With your net zone shot, you should be VERY close to completing your "tactical 10."

Therefore, you should hit the type of shot designed to beat your opponent, not the type that can only encourage him to lose to you. Generally, avoid drop shots and lobs on your third shot. While these are valuable to help set up a point, both are softly hit and easy to run down. Moreover, when you choose one of these, you ignore your big advantage: net weaponry. (In the next lesson, we will discuss the strength of your weaponry and how to use it to finish off an opponent from the net zone.)

Pitching In To Help

Although poaching is still several lessons in the future, this is a good time to take a moment and set the stage for what's to come. Since we've been talking about the entrance shot, I should mention the reluctance I've seen among some players to even get involved in the point if they're not the one hitting the entrance shot. DON'T BE RELUCTANT! Learn how to help out.

Just as you wouldn't expect a friend to do everything to pull dinner together, don't expect your partner to hit all three shots during a point. If your partner has just served, for example, your team has two more shots. Plan on helping with one of them or you may as well take a seat on the sideline. That doesn't mean you should get into every point by poaching, but keep your eyes open for opportunities. More about this later.

To Summarize

Plan to finish your opponents off, on schedule, in three hits. By progressing from an entrance shot, to a transition shot, to a net zone shot, you and your partner need to inflict enough damage (T10) on the opponents to win the point.

Point Control System Drill

You may do this drill alone, but with a partner, more accurate observations can be made. During actual game play, observe and assess the quality of your three types of shots. Perhaps, despite a strong serve, you aren't winning your service games. Are you missing your transitions? Or, maybe your shot from the net zone is not damaging enough. Use this drill to assess your strengths and weaknesses.

Also, make some notes on the "tactical 10" concept. Are you anywhere close to winning the point at the end of your team's third shot? Are you aggressively claiming you want to beat your opponents, but hitting a lob from the baseline for your third shot? Or are you blasting your entrance shots, trying to immediately force an error, rather than building toward the third shot? If you're doing these things, how does it affect your consistency?

Awareness is the first component of change. The goal of the foregoing exercise is to enhance your awareness of the strength of the three-shot concept and what it can bring to your game. But, even if you simply use this lesson to expose what you didn't know, you've moved one step closer to the game you're capable of playing.

Congratulations!

You've now completed the lesson on the three primary types of shots and are ready to build on this knowledge by moving to the next lesson.

Lesson 7 - Choose Your Weapon

How To End The Point

Objective

The number of shots needed to win any given point is in inverse proportion to the amount of damage you're doing with those shots. In this lesson, you'll learn exactly what tactical weapons are available to damage the opponents and how to keep the opponents from turning those same weapons on you.

"The Weapons"

There are three tactical weapons in doubles. For ease of understanding, I've labeled them "power," "angle" and "reaction time." Because they are all enhanced by your proximity to the net, it's best to think in terms of taking your third shot in the net zone. Each successive shot in your three-shot series should be more damaging than the one preceding, with the net-zone shot completing your flurry of tactical devastation.

Using "Power"

Power, for tennis purposes, is said to exist when the ball is hit with great force toward a target. Players must remember, however, that to readily use the "power weapon," the ball's path to the target must not be obstructed by the net. This implies certain restrictions on shot-making. For example, if you are in mid-court faced with a shoulder-high ball, you can see that all shots hit directly to the front of the opponent's court are blocked by the net. (Diagram #12)

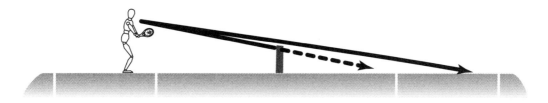

From mid-court even a shoulder height ball cannot be hit with power
because the net blocks shots to all but the deepest court targets.

Diagram #12

Since you can only use "power shots" when hitting to the deeper court, to reach the front portion of the court you have to cut back on the power and arc the ball over the net.

But, as you close in on the net, you can hit that same shoulder-high ball to much more of the opponent's court, and you no longer have to ease up on the power or arc the ball in. (Diagram #13)

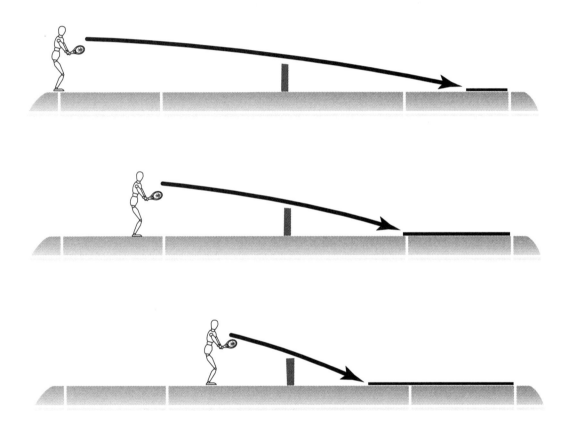

As you get closer to the net there is
more court available to your power weapon.

Diagram #13

An easy way to determine if you can use the power weapon is to draw a straight line from the point of contact with the ball to your target on the surface of the opponents' court. If the ball would have to go through the net to hit its mark, the power weapon is compromised. It is generally uncompromised and available if that same straight line would clear the net and hit the target. (Diagram #14)

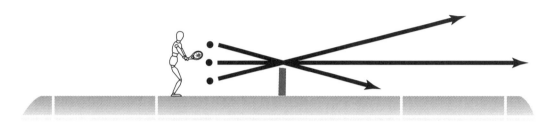

Draw a straight line from your point of contact to a point over the net.
If the line never hits court surface, your power weapon is compromised.
Refuse to cut power and your shot will follow the solid path.

Diagram #14

Using "Angle"

Angle can be defined as your ability to make your opponents' court "larger" by increasing the area they must cover to stay in the point. Steadily, as you move closer to the net, sharper angles are available to you and your partner and you have forced the opponents to cover a "larger" court. (Diagram #15)

The best way to exploit angle against an opponent is to hit crosscourt. Deuce to deuce, ad to ad. You minimize the effectiveness of angle when you hit down the line or down the middle. (Diagram #16)

Using "Reaction Time"

A quote like "time makes all things possible," really epitomizes this weapon. Lack of reaction time is really what destroys opponents. In a way, you could say that all three weapons boil down to just this one: "reaction time weapon."

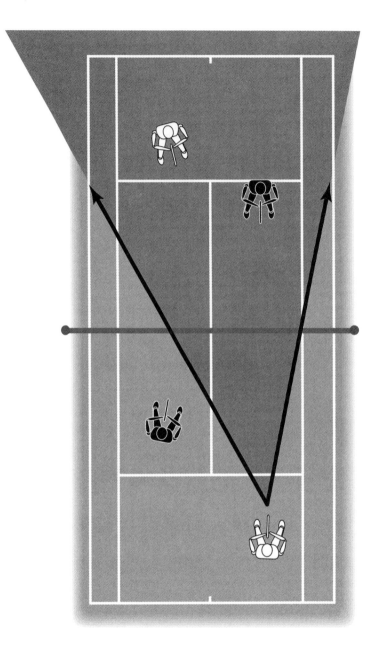

"Angle" makes the opponents cover more area.

Diagram #15

 Lesson 7 - Choose Your Weapon

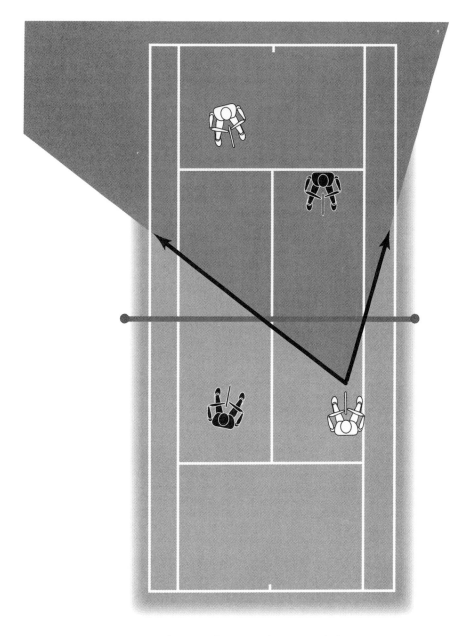

As you advance to the net, angle increases.
Crosscourt provides more angle than down-the-line.

Diagram #16

You know you've beaten your opponents with "power" when they weren't able to handle the speed of the ball you hit. Why couldn't they handle it? Because they didn't have enough *time* to get the racquet properly positioned to hit to their chosen target.

You know you've beaten the opponents with "angle" when they didn't have enough *time* to chase your shot to the side fence.

The availability of reaction time is simply a function of speed and distance. If you increase the speed of your shot (power weapon), you shorten the reaction time available to your opponents. Increasing hitting speed, of course, is easiest when you have a high ball to hit, and most difficult on low balls.

You can also reduce reaction time by moving toward the net, thereby decreasing the distance between yourself and your opponents. When you use this approach to the reaction time weapon your consistency isn't threatened, as it would be if you simply tried to use power to blast the ball through from the baseline. (Diagram #17)

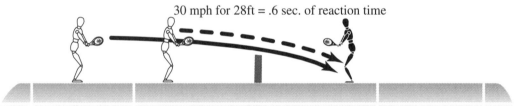

30 mph for 28ft = .6 sec. of reaction time

30 mph for 44ft = 1 sec. of reaction time

Reaction time is a function of speed and distance. When you
move closer to the net rather than hit harder, consistency isn't threatened.

Diagram #17

To most effectively use your reaction-time weapon, hit to the opening on the alley side of your closest opponent. Because he's closest, he has the least time to react to your shot. When you use the middle for this purpose, you may beat the net player, but the middle is sometimes shared by his deeper partner who has more time to react.

The "Double-Edged Sword"

Now that you understand how to use the three tactical weapons of power, angle and reaction time, let's learn how to take them away so that your opponents can't effectively use them on you.

Minimizing The Opponent's "Power"

To take the power weapon from your opponents' arsenal, keep the net between their point of contact with the ball and their target so they don't have a straight line to their target. This means you have to keep the ball low when hitting to them. That way, they are forced to play either a touch shot back to your feet (with very little pace), or risk popping the ball up, giving *your* team access to the power weapon. (Diagram #18)

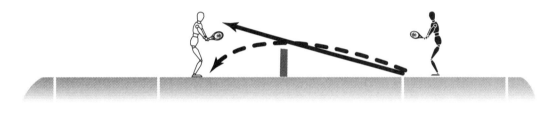

To shut off the opponent's power weapon, keep the ball low.
This forces him to play a touch shot back or pop the ball up.

Diagram #18

Your decision to keep the ball low is based on your skill and your opponents' court positions. If they stay back, or get stuck in the transition zone, hitting to their feet is easier than if they've taken an aggressive net zone position in front of the one-third mark. Still, keep the ball low whenever possible. You want to restrict their use of the power weapon, particularly when they're in the net zone, so you may preserve your own net zone presence.

Reducing The Opponent's "Angle"

The only way to weaken the opponents' angle weapon is to get them away from the net. This may not be easy, however, since most knowledgeable doubles players will fight for the net position at almost any cost, in hopes of preserving their "weapon-rich" offensive positions.

Less tactically-savvy players, on the other hand, will back away from the net at the slightest provocation. This, of course, shrinks their available angles and simultaneously makes their feet vulnerable as targets, which minimizes their use of the power weapon as well. The only pseudo-effective way to take the angle weapon from a team at the net (a team that knows the value of its position) is to try to back them off with a lob. The reason I say "pseudo-effective" is because, while you do take away their angle weapon, you risk giving them the power weapon in exchange by tossing them a lob. If your opponents have strong overheads, perhaps the exchange is not a great idea. You have to decide in an instant if the trade-off is in your best interests.

Taking Away The "Reaction Time" Weapon

To repeat, reaction time is primarily a function of speed and distance. To increase the reaction time your team has available to field your opponents' shots, there are three factors that must be considered:

You must take away their power weapon. If you keep the ball low, they'll have to reduce pace and arc the ball over the net to their target. This slower-moving ball will give your team more to-the-ball closure time, which will keep you from feeling reactive.

A second way to increase your reaction time is to increase the distance between yourselves and your opponents. It would be to your advantage to get *them* to back away from the net. However, if you can't manage this, be aware that if you back up, you do increase your reaction time, but at a price. You also open up the angles to your opponents and a savvy net team will take advantage of this. (Diagram #19)

Most high-level opponents won't back away from the net and give you more time to deal with their shots, so you'll need a good lob (Lesson 11). And, once again, lobbing is a trade-off, because of the risk of an overhead reply.

As you may have noticed, I can teach you how to minimize the effectiveness of specific weapons your opponents might use for a given situation. But, if they're really savvy net players, they'll just substitute another and do their damage with it. I suggest you do the same.

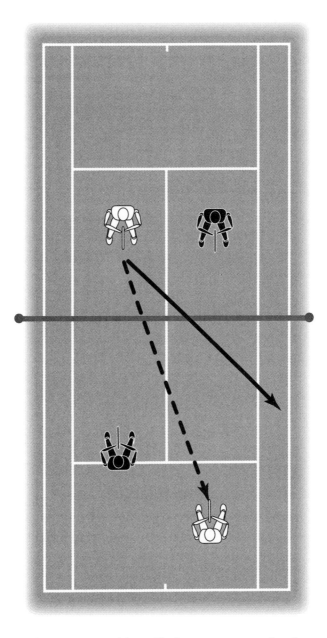

A deeper court position will give you more reaction time,
but make you more susceptible to angle.

Diagram #19

Special "Reaction Time" Note

My suggestion is to make your strokes as short as possible as you get closer to the net. This will help make best use of the available reaction time. Some volley techniques require more time than others. If you often feel the balls are coming *at* you rather than *to* you, this is most likely because your volley technique takes too much time. Doubles requires a shorter volley motion than singles due to the shorter distances between players. Get some help in developing a nice compact volley technique. There's nothing worse than stepping in to get a volley and discovering instead that the volley got you!

To Summarize

There are three tactical weapons: power, angle, and reaction time. All three are enhanced by your presence in the net zone. When your team is hitting its third shot, it should be using at least one of these weapons to end the point. When your opponents try to diminish the effectiveness of one of the weapons, substitute another.

Point Control System Drill

Schedule a practice match in which you and your partner will quickly state after each point how it was won or lost. Which weapons were used? Notice whether you won the point with a great angle, or because you took on the player with the least reaction time. Perhaps you combined angle with power to reach your "Tactical 10". Notice which weapons you're using (if any!) when you and your partner are in the net zone. Are you hitting the openings? Notice and discuss the effectiveness of the weapons you're using.

Congratulations!

You've completed the lesson on net weapons. You now posses clear knowledge of how tactical damage is done and you're fully equipped to move on to the next lesson.

Lesson 8 - What Are They Up To?

How To Anticipate Your Opponents' Every Move

Objective

"Anticipation" is defined as the ability to predict what will happen next. This is a vital skill that will develop naturally when the opponents avoid you by hitting the openings. While there are many factors in anticipating which opening they will choose, the objective of this lesson is to teach you how court positioning and weaponry affects your opponents' shot selections so you can gain advanced warning.

Proactive vs. Reactive

Most players are content to wait until the opponents hit the ball and then react. Consequently, anticipation is something they've heard of but don't actually practice.

Think of it this way: You have an anticipatory program on the hard drive of your internal tennis computer. Its job is to give you advance warning concerning the opponent's targets. The more points you play with this program running, the more reliable the answer it gives because it has more data upon which to formulate an answer.

However, the computer is not automatically switched on. You must do it yourself. You must request to know where the opponent's shot is headed *before* he strikes the ball. That's what it means to "anticipate." If you ask after the opponent strikes the ball, the computer assumes you didn't want advance warning so it runs its "emergency reaction" program. This program may be sufficient if the opponent is hitting right *to* you or you're very fast on your feet. But if the opponent knows to hit the openings, and the speed of his shot exceeds your foot speed, the "emergency reaction" program will not be adequate to enable you to reach the incoming shots.

I'm not suggesting that anticipation is everything and being reactive is bad. You need both to be a complete player. This can be seen if you examine what it takes to run a business today. Companies must be proactive. To thrive in today's competitive business environment, they have to look ahead, they have to anticipate trends. But they must also retain enough flexibility to react to swiftly changing market conditions.

The question business owners and tennis players must ask is: "How can I be both at the same time?" Unfortunately, the answer is that you can't be. So, you do your best. You strive to stay ahead of events, to anticipate what is developing. You're proactive. If your interpretation proves wrong, you instantly react.

Intention - The Foundation For Anticipation

Earlier we defined anticipation as the ability to predict what is going to happen next. If we add an opponent to the equation, we can narrow the definition to "the ability to predict the opponent's target intention." You cannot anticipate accidents. This lesson, then, focuses on learning how to anticipate what target the opponent intends to hit.

What, Exactly, Are You To Anticipate?

Many players feel that to anticipate they must ask themselves the question: "Where is the opponent going to aim the ball?" A question like this could take a long time to answer; longer than you have in the split-second before the opponent strikes the ball. So let me help simplify.

There really is no need to anticipate balls already coming *to* you, so this lesson will help you distinguish how the opponent will attempt to *avoid* you. There are 3 ways to avoid you (and hit an opening). The opponent can either hit to your right, to your left, or lob over your head. All you have to do is anticipate which of these three directions the ball is going.

These directions are based on "your own world." This is because you and your partner each have your own anticipatory computers and they are running independently. It doesn't matter that the ball may be going crosscourt all the way to your partner's alley. It's still going to that side of you and that's all you need to know- left, right, or over *you*.

If you remember school, multiple choice questions were always easier and faster to answer than fill-in-the-blank! So ask, "Which way is it going?".. instead of "Where is it going?" Multiple choice...instead of fill in the blank. (Diagram #20)

Court Position Is #1

We learned about being "in position" in a previous lesson. What we didn't discuss is how being "in position" affects the opponents. One of the interesting observations

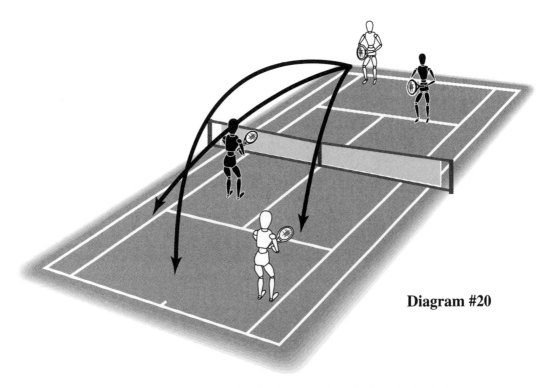

Diagram #20

Don't ask "Where is the ball going?" Instead, make it multiple choice:
"Is it headed to my right, left, or over my head?"

you'll make is that when your team is "in position" there is no opening that's any more appealing than another...they're all the same size. That's what it means to "bisect." Still, court position is the number one influence of the opponents' shot selections. Let's learn how this works.

Left / Right Dimension Influence

The opponents would rather hit to an opening than to you or your partner. When your team is out of bisection in the left/right dimension, it leaves an opening that is larger than the rest. It doesn't matter which one of you is "out of position," the fact is that there's an exaggerated opening. You should expect this opening to be strongly considered by the opponents. (Diagram #21)

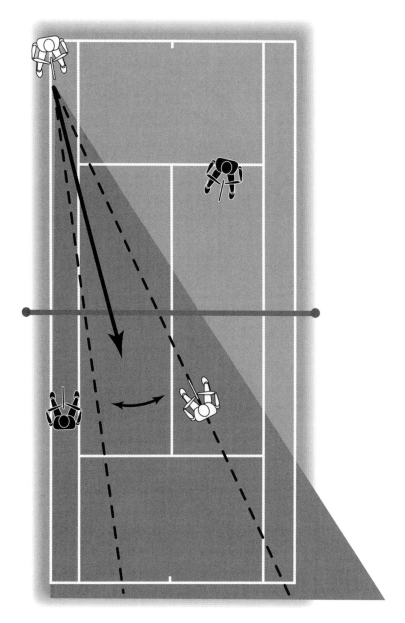

The ad court player is off his line of bisection
as he over-protects his alley. This creates an
opening down the middle.

Diagram #21

Front / Rear Dimension Influence

In a very basic sense, there is a direct relationship between your team's front/rear court position and how often your team will be lobbed. When you take a "neutral" position at the 1/3 mark, opponents who desire to beat you will try to keep the ball low (foot depth bounce point) and control the net zone. Opponents who have chosen to ask you to lose to them will most likely lob and take deeper positions. Either way, when you position yourselves neutrally in the front/rear dimension, the opponents will reveal their intended means to emerge victorious. Adjusting your positions will not only influence their desire to lob in the moment, but their overall tactics as well. (Diagram #22)

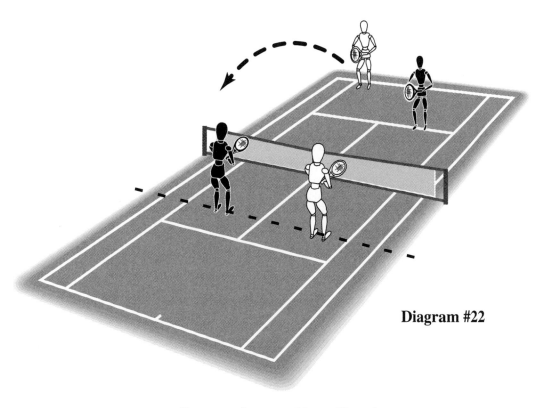

Diagram #22

Your neutral court positions will get the
opponents to reveal their tactical tendencies.

Weaponry is #2

Weaponry also plays a role in anticipation. Take a situation where one member of a team is playing from a deeper court position than his partner. The deeper player becomes the target for the opponents because, by being further from the net zone, his weapons are less potent than his partner's. This explains why service returns normally go back toward the server, despite the fact that both he and his partner are positioned on their respective lines of bisection. (Diagram #23)

The server's "less-weaponed" court position becomes the
basis for the server's net player to expect a return to his right.

Diagram #23

In working with pre-4.0 players, I find partners failing to understand how their court positions interrelate. Often a server will follow his serve in, and volley the crosscourt return back toward the receiver. He then transitions to the net zone and takes his proper position at the 1/3 mark, only to puzzle over his partner being lobbed. What this player should puzzle over is his team's failure to understand that it was their correct positions that created a situation wherein they should have anticipated a lob. (Diagram #24)

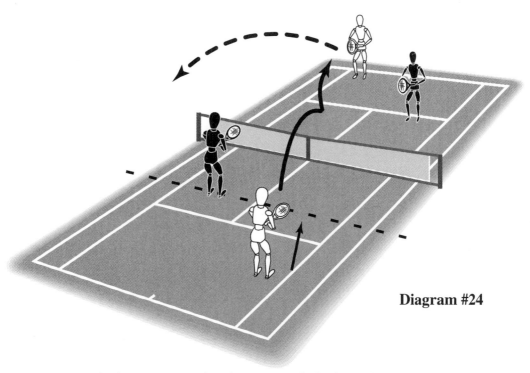

Diagram #24

As the server moves into the net zone eliminating a "less-weaponed" side of the court, even his neutrally positioned net player can be viewed as too close by a receiver who elected to stay back.

From the receiver's viewpoint, the server's net man was a threat from the start of the point because of his position in the net zone. Therefore, the receiver avoided the net man by returning crosscourt toward the server, who had fewer weapons. But, when the server moved into the net zone he added to his weaponry. The receiver then faced a balanced net zone threat and felt the only way he could get past it was to lob.

At this point players should be reminded that, with certain exceptions, the person being lobbed should back up and cover it. Otherwise the server will not be able to comfortably advance into the net zone. The ideal situation is for the team to be side by side in the net zone at whatever depth they feel tactically appropriate. It is less than ideal if the server, because of his partner's failure to anticipate and cover lobs, is forced to hang back in the transition zone. This exposes the server's feet as targets and gives his team no net zone representation on his half of the court. (Diagram #25)

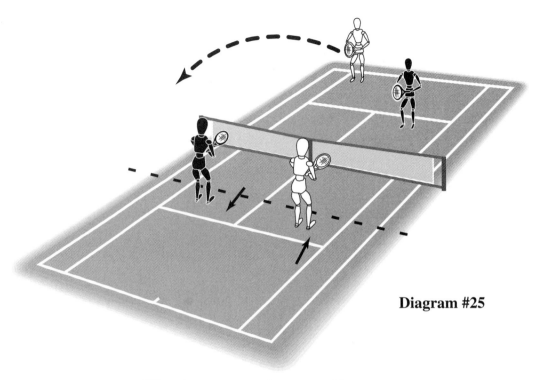

Diagram #25

When the server enters the net zone, his partner must
back up and take responsibility for any lobs over his head.

The Tactically Challenged

Players 4.0 and above usually have strong overheads and a good understanding of court position. As a result, they can severely punish teams that over-use lobs. Players below 4.0 are generally less-developed tactically. These pre-4.0 players, in their efforts to incorporate consistency into their games, may use lobs often, sometimes beyond the restraint of good tactics. Because anticipation is basically an understanding of logical probabilities, improbable tactics by the tactically-challenged can be difficult to anticipate.

To Summarize

Anticipate that your opponent will direct balls away from you most of the time. Your opponent has three choices of shots he can make to avoid hitting to you at the net: he can hit to your right, to your left, or over you. His choice of shot will be strongly influenced by your and your partner's court positions and available weaponry.

Point Control System Drill

This drill requires four players. Two players position themselves on the service line. The third player positions himself at mid-court directly behind this team. From here, he will feed balls to the fourth player who has taken a spot on the opposite baseline. (As you'll recall, there were three basic positions for the "in-position" lesson. In this instance, the solo player on the baseline should take a position in the deuce court alley). The objective of this drill is to have the baseline player recognize and hit to an opening deliberately created by the team at the net.

To begin, the net team confers and decides how one (or both) are to lure the baseline opponent to hit to the opening they are going to create. For example, let's say they elect to create an opening down the line from the baseline player. Though aware of proper positioning, when the feeder puts the ball into play, the net team moves to the 1/3 mark, but in an alignment that creates an opening. The baseline player spots the opening and tries to hit it. Initially, volley attempts shouldn't be made (no to-the-ball closures). Just create the openings with your in-position closures and split-step. Let the baseline player spot and hit them. Make a note of when you must make your in-position closure if the hitter is to see you. The sooner you both can complete your in-position closures and split-steps, the more certain the baseline opponent will be of the target you are luring him to. If you're too slow, he'll be guessing where the opening is. (Hint: Finish your in-position closure before the feed crosses the net.) To truly understand this drill, players must play all roles. After ten attempts, the teams should change places. (Diagram #26)

As a second level to the drill, go ahead and step into the openings and volley. This change will provide practice of the in-position closure, split-step, and to-the-ball closure. (Diagram #27)

Congratulations!

You've successfully installed anticipatory software to your personal tennis computer. You're now fully equipped to move on to the final four lessons where all eight lessons will be interrelating.

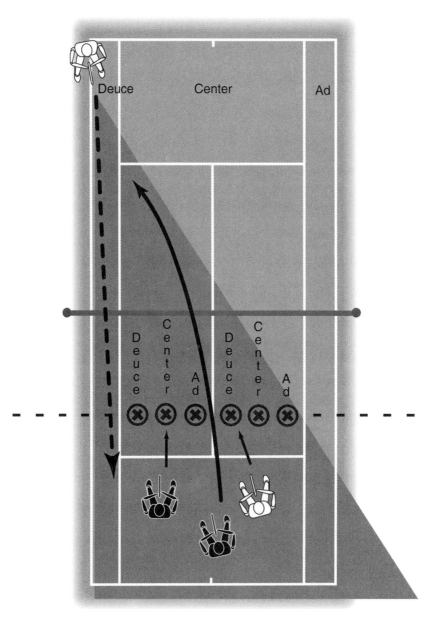

You and your partner decide which one of you will improperly bisect
to lure the opponent to hit the opening you deliberately create. In this
example, the ad court player is creating an opening in his alley.

Diagram #26

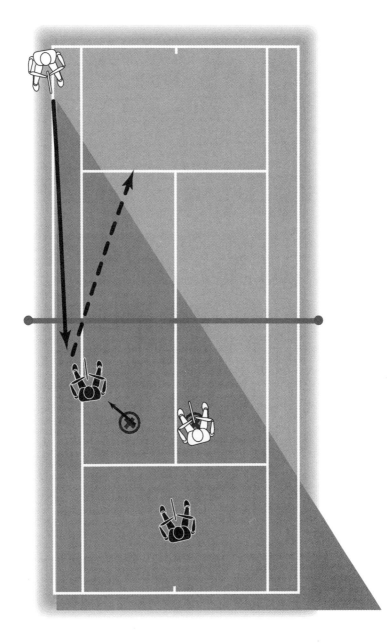

After everyone has had several chances to see and hit the openings,
practice "to-the-ball" closures as the ball is moving toward your team.

Diagram #27

Let's Take Inventory

Before we begin the final lessons, let's take a moment to review the foundation you've built (even though the cement is still wet!).

You know you have two options for emerging the victor in a match, and a three shot series is considered consistent.

You know where to be on the court when the opponent is hitting.

You know to hit the openings ... not the opponents.

You also know how to flow with the movement of the ball through the three zones.

You know what weapons are available and how to use them.

And, you know how to anticipate your opponents' shots.

Now watch how simply these concepts interrelate to win points!

Lesson 9 - The Lead Off

How to Win Your Service Games

Objective

As your doubles game develops, you'll reach a point (if you haven't already) where you'll need to "hold serve." You'll recognize this point when it's becoming increasingly difficult to break your opponents' serves.

In this lesson you will learn how to begin in the "entrance zone" with the serve, move through the "transition zone" with your first volley, and end the point in the "net zone." The goal being to inflict enough damage with your tactical weapons over the course of these three shots to win the point and hold serve.

It's Time To Serve And Volley

Often at the 3.0 to 3.5 level you can get away with serving and staying back because the opponents haven't yet learned to be consistent and to use their net positions to true advantage. A server can hang back, buying reaction time, and merely ask the opponents to lose to him by throwing up lobs or hitting ground strokes. But, sooner or later, you'll need to develop a serve and volley game if you are to progress.

For 4.0 and above players, it becomes increasing difficult to hold serve by staying back. Although still possible (with a sound understanding of weaponry, willing opponents and a little luck), I strongly suggest you abandon any inclination to stay back and set your sights on ending the point in the net zone.

Serving With A Plan

As you step-up to the baseline, intend to get your first serve in rather than rely on your spare. Begin by choosing a target. Do you intend to serve down the middle, pull the receiver wide, or go into the body? Begin from a court position that permits all three options. Standing out wide (toward the sideline) will make wide serves easier but limit your ability to serve down the middle. Similarly, standing toward the middle will help you serve down the middle but decrease your ability to pull the receiver wide. Begin neutrally so you don't tip off the receiver and take a moment to feel the flow of the three shot progression you're about to make toward the net.

Proactive Beginnings

After you choose what you're going to do with the serve, but before delivering it, think a moment about your opponent's return of serve. He has basically three options: crosscourt, down the line, or a lob. Think about which one you expect (server's partner should be doing the same). This not only flips on your anticipatory computer and ensures pro-activity, but readies you for your transition shot. (Diagram #28)

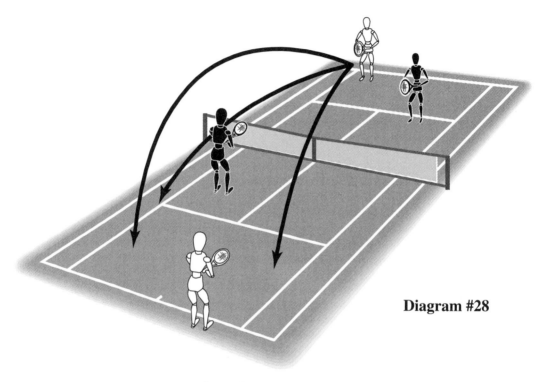

Diagram #28

Before delivering the serve, think
about how the receiver will reply.

The Toss Makes a Difference

The toss is the switch that turns on "moving forward." Since we're focusing on "winning" points we're headed for the net zone where the weapons are. So, the toss needs to move out in front to help you begin your momentum toward the net. A toss in front leads you into the court the way a quarterback leads a receiver with a touchdown pass. This makes serving and flowing toward the net an easy process as you exit the serve moving forward and into a gentle run.

Moving Into The Court

While the ball is headed toward its target, stay relaxed and focused while using your "in-position" closure to move forward to the transition zone. Advance quickly but not so quickly that you forget your split-step.

Split-Step

Split-step as the receiver is about to strike the ball. This split-step will allow you to change direction, for example, to cover a lob over your partner's head. Since the split-step is a "when" not a "where," YOU DON'T HAVE TO BE IN FRONT OF THE SERVICE LINE when you do it. I've seen some very effective transitional volleys made by players who practically walked in following their serves. Take your time and opt for quality.

In fact, if you're too fast in moving forward, smart receivers (like you!) will simply lob your partner, forcing you to slow down your closure on the net. They will continue to do this until your feet are a visible target for the return. If your opponents are worthy, half-volleys and low volleys are unavoidable. But, your well-timed split-step will help you handle these smoothly.

Transition Shot

As the service return heads toward you, move forward to meet the incoming ball with your "to the ball closure." Your weapons are most potent at the net, so moving forward not only enhances your weaponry but restricts the opponents' access to your feet on subsequent hits.

Accept the fact that serve and volleying means you're going to face hitting up on some first volleys. Worthy receivers will routinely hit the ball low and crosscourt, targeting your feet as they try to eliminate the power weapon from your transition. Learn to take these shots in stride and you'll be paving the way toward the highest levels. So, expect the low balls and be pleasantly surprised when they err and give you a nice high volley.

There are really only two valid targets for your transition shot: crosscourt toward the receiver or down the alley of the receiver's net man. It helps here if you have some idea ahead of time concerning what you're going to do with that first volley. Most players hit back to the receiver (fewer weapons). Whatever your choice, your main objective should be to keep the ball low. This takes your opponent's power weapon out of the point and, simultaneously, increases your team's reaction-time (shutting down their power weapon is imperative if you are to safely advance to the net zone). (Diagram #29)

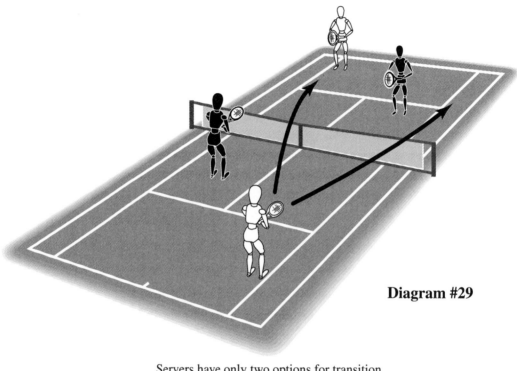

Diagram #29

Servers have only two options for transition
and should have both in their repertoire.
Remember to keep the ball low.

It's difficult to consistently inflict major damage with your first volley. If you've kept the ball low you've done well. If you've kept it low *and* into an opening, you're a genius! Even with a high ball, you won't be capable of consistently inflicting major tactical damage until you're comfortably into the net zone and executing your third shot.

Net Zone Shot

When you've hit your transition shot and the ball is moving toward your opponent, use your "in-position" closure to move toward the net zone. Remember that the position you take in the net zone will affect your opponent's shot selection. Position yourself well in the left/right dimension and be certain that you're close enough to the net that the opponents can't hit your feet as they can when you're transitioning. If you feel their desire is to keep the ball low, split-step in neutral net position and then close to intercept the incoming ball before it gets below the height of the net. But if you feel your transition shot may induce a lob, use a slightly deeper split-step than neutral (1/3 mark) to discourage it. (Diagram #30)

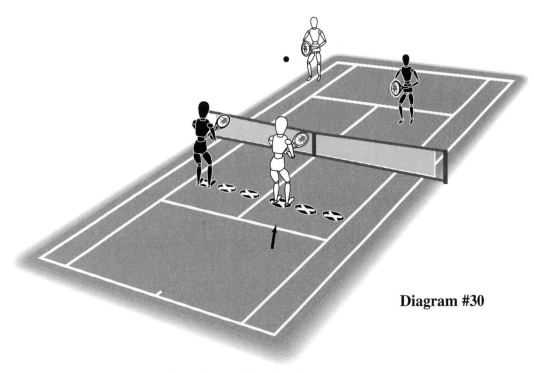

Diagram #30

After the transition shot, both you and your
partner take net zone positions that are appropriate
for the hitting opponent's court position.

Make the most of your net zone opportunity by picking on the alley of the opponent with the least reaction time or hitting an angle to win the point. (Diagram #31)

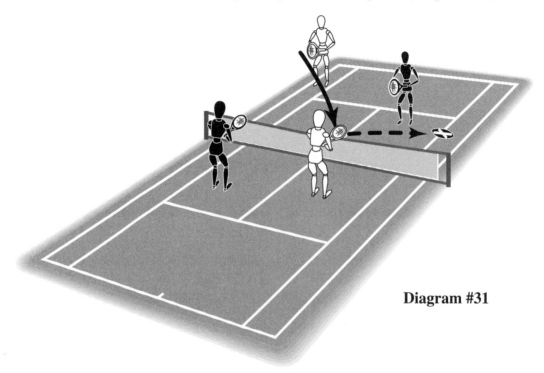

Diagram #31

In the net zone, maximize your use of reaction-time
weapon by picking on the alley of the closer opponent.

Handling The Lobbed Service Return

This topic has been intentionally ignored in this lesson. While this skill can be very important to holding serve (especially if your net player doesn't cover his own lobs once you enter the net zone), it is covered in Lesson 11. In fact, not only will you learn to survive this rather challenging situation, you will emerge in control without losing your net zone representation, still on schedule to a three-hit "tactical 10."

Did You Do This Alone?

In the lesson on poaching, you'll learn more about the role of the server's partner in winning service games. For now, know that at the highest level poachers play a major role in teams holding serve. In fact, some feel that is isn't the server who "holds serve," it is, rather, the server's partner.

To Summarize

Choose a target for your serve and anticipate the type of return. Move through your transition shot, keeping the ball low so you can enter the net zone and end the point with your weapons.

Point Control System Drill

This drill requires two players. You and your partner take positions on opposite sides of the net in either the deuce or the ad court. One of you will serve, the other receive. The objective is for the server to practice transitioning to the net by linking the entrance, transition and net-zone shots. Hit the ball right *to* each other and do not play the point out beyond a six shot exchange. Serve, hit the transitional volley, then volley from the 1/3 spot (or closer to the net). Switch roles and court sides until both of you have served and returned from the deuce and the ad courts. Be nice and steady, remembering your split-steps and closing in on your volleys.

It is extremely important that you find comfort and confidence in linking these three shots. Connecting the serve, transitional volley and net zone volley is necessary if you are to blend consistency and tactical aggressiveness. Your ability to hit three shots in a row, while closing in to the net, is your ticket to the unending road of advancement and the basis for feeling secure while playing points.

Congratulations!

Now that you've learned how to link three shots together to hold serve, you're ready to move on to the next lesson.

Lesson 10 - The Reply

How To Break Your Opponent's Serve

Objective

The return of serve is regarded by many as the most important shot in the game since it is the first step in breaking the opponent's serve. If you are to win matches you must eventually "break serve." In the last lesson, you learned that the server's objective is to use his serve, his transitional volley and the net-zone volley to win points. In this lesson, you will learn how to neutralize a serving team's advantage.

The Server's Advantage

The serving team's advantage derives from the fact that they get to hit their entrance shot first, permitting them to get to the net zone first. Consequently, to overcome this advantage, the receiving team must focus on tactics that will enable them to have first use of the net zone weapons.

The Starting Position

As you learned in earlier lessons, all court positions have two coordinates: (1) the front/rear dimension and (2) the left/right dimension. The starting point I recommend in the front/rear dimension is just slightly inside the baseline. You then customize it to suit the quality of the serve. For example, if the serve is soft and short, you stand closer. Or, if you find you need more reaction time because of the strength of the serve, back up a little (but keep in mind that the farther you start from the net, the farther you are from your most potent weapons). Increasing your distance from the net zone to buy reaction time is an uncertain trade-off. If you back up too far, you open up the server's angle. On the other hand, you will have more time to reach the ball. Think through each situation and adjust the front/rear dimension until it meets your needs.

The starting point I recommend for the left/right dimension is in the bisection of the server's available court. Watch where the server positions himself to begin serving, then stand in the middle of the best wide serve he could hit and his best possible down- the-middle serve. He'll probably have a pattern. Adjust your stance once you detect it. You should also adjust your position to hide specific return weaknesses. For example, if your backhand return is not as strong as you'd like, make that target a bit smaller for the server (lure him to hit to your strength). However, begin neutrally and learn the server's tendencies before you make any target adjustments. (Diagram #32)

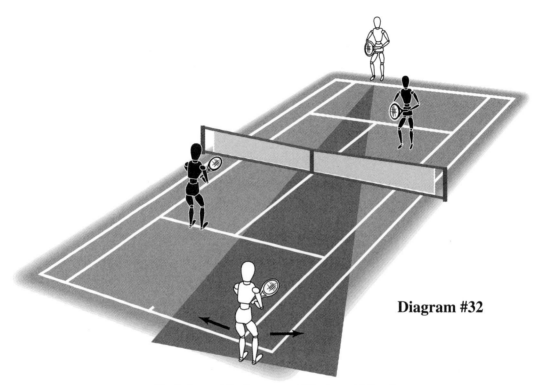

Diagram #32

Begin by positioning yourself in the middle of
the server's available court. Later, adjust your starting
position left or right to control the server's placement.

What Are Your Return Options?

Assuming you're unwilling to hit directly to the net man, you have three primary return-of-serve targets: (1) crosscourt (2) down the line and (3) lob. As a general rule, 80% of service returns are crosscourt, 10% down the line and 10% lobbed. The crosscourt return is the backbone of the receiving game because the server is deeper in the court and, therefore, has less-potent weapons. (Diagram #33)

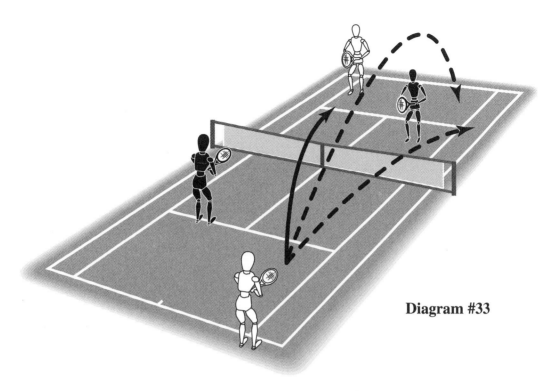

Diagram #33

Although three returns are possible,
crosscourt returns are the key to breaking serve.

Choosing Your Target

Since not all returns are available from the different receiving positions, the server narrows your choices based on the target he selects for his serve. For example, if he pulls you wide into the alley, you can hit crosscourt, down the line or lob. But, if he serves down the middle, hitting down the line is very difficult. That restricts you to crosscourt or lob.

Most strong receivers choose their target before the serve has been hit. And even the most improvisational players usually narrow the choice to one or two targets. For example, "If he serves me wide, I'm going down the line. If he serves down the middle, I'm hitting crosscourt." The server's actions following the serve offer another opportunity. If he has been rocketing into the net with no split-step, his partner is ripe for a lob. Focus on what you want as an outcome and don't be distracted from this goal.

Don't wait to see what the server's partner is doing before you choose your target. That gives the server's partner too much control over your service returns. If you make your choice *before* the serve has been hit, you'll find execution much easier.

Will You Hit The Ball Or Will The Ball Hit You?

It's very important on service returns that you are the "hitter" and not the "hittee." Don't wait for the ball. Step forward, prepared for the return. This activates the aggressiveness needed to overcome the server's advantage.

Begin by taking a large step forward (in-position closure) when the server makes his ball toss. As he's hitting the ball, make your split-step, ready to move in any direction. Go to meet it with your to-the-ball closure. Don't plant yourself and wait... be the hitter. Expect that it may not be coming right to you, so you go forward to intercept it. This will get you to the net more quickly, decrease the time your opponents have to reach your return, and enable you to more accurately hit your target. It's no coincidence that this return-of-serve procedure is a condensed version of your lesson on how to flow with the action on the court (forward, split-step, forward).

Breaking Serve With The Crosscourt Return

The crosscourt return will be the backbone of your receiving game because the distance the ball must travel provides you with enough in-position closure time to move forward into the transition zone.

The objective here is to minimize the server's weapons and make his transition more challenging. Keep the ball low. Bounce it near his feet as he attempts to flow through the transition zone. Done this way, the net comes between his point of contact and his available targets, limiting the use of his power weapon (which increases the amount of time available for your to-the-ball closure).

The server will attempt to transition behind a low ball into one of your openings. Success will make him difficult, but not impossible, to break. Short of your partner poaching off of your return (Lesson 12), which would jump your team from entrance shot to net zone shot in two hits, you must try to make your return your transition. If you can do this, you've advanced more quickly to the net than the server. Once there, you use your angle, power and reaction-time weapons to win the point. (Diagram #34)

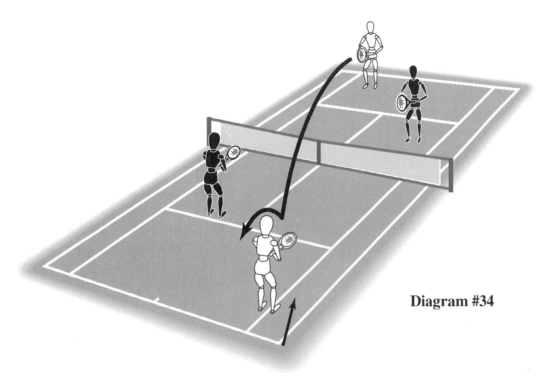

Diagram #34

Move forward to meet the serve. If you can make your
return a transition rather than an entrance shot, you can
often beat the server to the net zone.

If the server stays back, he's letting you jump ahead in the three-shot cycle. Return serve as deeply as you can. If he doesn't want to transition to the net zone, don't encourage him by hitting a short ball. Let him stay back, hoping you'll "lose" to his team. THERE IS NOTHING NICER THAN AN OPPONENT WHO IS NOT TRYING TO BEAT YOU!

Still, even though your deep return gives you enough in-position closure time, it's doubtful the server will let you get all the way to the net zone. Watch for the lob. Be prepared. Split-step at the service line and ask yourself, "Is he the kind of player who will try to "power weapon" through me from the baseline? Or will he play "please lose to me"? Which choice gives your team a consistency advantage? If the server's partner holds his net position and you aim for his alley, you'll have a reaction-time weapon. And, if the server stays back, he leaves an angle open on his side. You have court advantage, so take your time and remember to use your weapons. (Diagram #35)

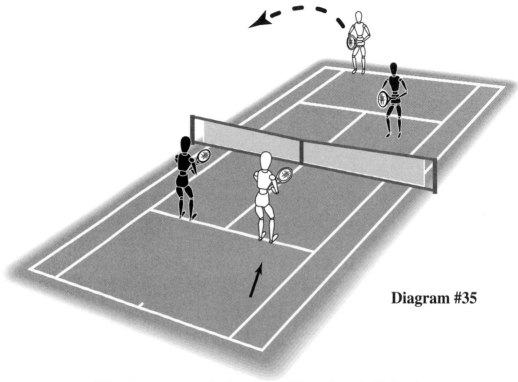

Diagram #35

When the server stays back, expect a "Please Lose To Me" style.
You and your partner should take positions on the service line
despite an abundance of in-position closure time.

The Lob Return

In several circumstances, a lob return is a wise choice. For example, if you can't seem to get your return down to the server's shoe tops. Perhaps he closes too quickly to the net or his net man is poaching well enough to protect his server's feet. The bottom line is: if you don't like your results with your crosscourt return, try lobbing.

Note the starting position of the opposing net player. If he's crowding the net and your crosscourt isn't producing the desired result, he's leaving your escape hatch open. Your goal in lobbing him is to force the server to play a second entrance shot (allowing your team to transition first). (Diagram #36)

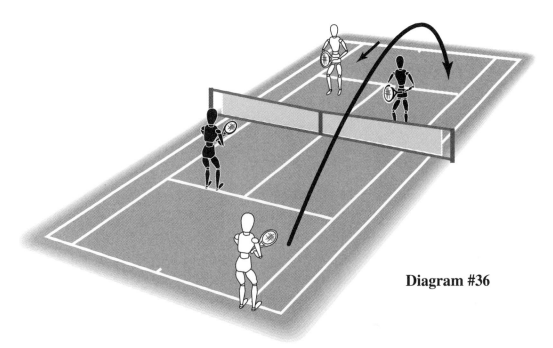

Diagram #36

When the server's feet aren't available for the
crosscourt return and/or the server's partner takes
an initial stance too close to the net... use your lob.

You should choose the lob before the serve is hit, then move forward just as you would if you were hitting a crosscourt return. Deception is a major factor in determining whether the lob makes it untouched over the net man.

If successful, this once again jumps you ahead in the three shot flow and challenges the serving team's advantage. Treat the server, who is covering the lob and bailing out his partner, just as you did in the previous example, when he chose to stay back.

Mixing Things Up With Down-The-Line Returns

Although this is the return of choice for the "one-shot" player, the down-the-line return is best used only as a tactic to keep an active poacher in check. It is most effective when the server's partner has an aggressive starting position and the serve is wide.

Begin your return by moving into the ball as you would on any other return. Aim a comfortable distance into the alley and don't assume it will always be a winner. Successful net players may volley your return down the middle between you and your partner. So, unless you plan on being a "one-shot" player, prepare to come out of the alley and break toward the middle. (Diagram #37)

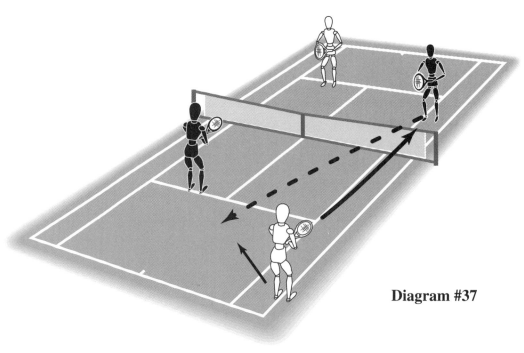

Diagram #37

When using the down-the-line return, don't stand and admire your shot hoping for a winner. Instead, move toward the middle to handle a possible reply from the opposing net player.

The down-the-line entrance shot is a departure from your goal of consistency. It's comparable to the server attempting aces. Granted, it employs your reaction-time weapon as you're attempting to inflict extreme damage, but it's risky and should be used sparingly.

To Summarize

Use your starting position to influence the serve. Choose one of three returns before the serve is delivered and stick to it. Focus mainly on the crosscourt and use the lob and the down-the-line for variety. Step forward to be the hitter, split-step and move forward again to meet the serve. The key to breaking serve lies in your team's ability to jump ahead of the serving team in the three shot schedule.

Point Control System Drill

This drill requires two players. One player will serve, the other return. Place a chair or other marker on the court to signify the server's partner and practice hitting all three returns (crosscourt, down-the-line and lob) from both the deuce and the ad courts. Move into the returns and continue toward the net, just as you would if you were in a real game looking for a transition shot. Switch positions so you can return your partner's serve.

Just a little side note here: LEARN TO RETURN FROM BOTH THE DEUCE AND THE AD COURTS so you can be a more versatile player. It's okay to have a preference, but I highly recommend you learn to hit from both courts.

Congratulations!

You've completed the lesson on return of serve and you're ready to build on this knowledge by moving on to the next lesson.

Lesson 11 - Crush It!

How To Hit And Handle The Lob Game

Objective

Used properly, the lob is an extremely effective shot to have in your arsenal. Your team's ability to lob well and to respond to lobs can be the difference between winning and losing. In this lesson you will increase your understanding of lobs, learn when and how to use them, and also how to handle your opponents' lobs.

The Types Of Lob

There are three types of lob: defensive, offensive and unintentional. Defensive lobs are used when you need time to recover. Typically, their trajectory is very high and their target is somewhat vague, because the lobber is in trouble. If you need more in-position closure time because you've been pulled out of position, the defensive lob can be the tool to get the job done.

Less-skilled players will sometimes hit "unintentional" lobs. The racket face accidentally opens (probably due to lack of reaction time), and up goes the ball. Occasionally, these skim over the opponent and create the illusion of a great offensive lob. The good news for opponents is that these lobs begin to disappear as the player develops his skills. The bad news for opponents is that they are replaced by deliberate offensive lobs, which are much more damaging.

This lesson is primarily about the offensive lob. It's used most often to back opponents off the net when their weaponry is too potent (in front of the neutral net position). Done well, the low trajectory of the offensive lob should quickly clear the net players.

Lobs, Your Future And The "Please Lose To Me" Player

The lob world can be a very emotional area for many players. I often hear horror stories of how a team was lobbed to death. As a matter of fact, I've had people tell me they refuse to play with certain players anymore, because all they do is lob. But, frankly, handling lobbers emotionally is often harder than handling them on the court.

And, while this lesson is not intended to teach you how to beat the career "please lose to me" types, I do have a few suggestions that may change some of your thinking concerning the lob.

Many pre-4.0 players have underdeveloped overheads. Consequently, there is great temptation at this level to use the lob as a means to frustrate the opponents and ask them to lose to you. In fact, this is a source of great fun and amusement for many players! Although there's nothing inherently wrong with this, if you desire to progress to the 4.0-5.0 levels, you're becoming your own worst enemy.

The lob has very limited usage at the higher levels because players have strong overheads and welcome the opportunity to access their power weapon. These same players advance to the net zone and use their tactical weapons to *beat* the opponents. They won't base their primary hopes for victory on the possibility of the opponents *losing* to them. With this in mind, let's do some reasoning.

When To Lob

Remember: your goal is to end the point in three shots. This criterion provides a good balance between consistency and aggressiveness. By the third shot, you expect to have done enough tactical damage to win the point (tactical 10). You have an "entrance" shot, a "transition" shot and a "net" shot with which to do this. If you're going to hit a lob and still fall within your three-shot guidelines, it must be hit upon entrance, during transition, or at the net.

To highlight the reasoning here, let's look at the third shot (the net shot), and work our way back to the beginning of the point to see how the lob fits into the picture. You've decided you have only three shots to make the point. Now, imagine a lob as your third shot. How good are your chances of winning the point? (Selecting a lob as a winner at this juncture is like having time for only one more ride at Disney World and using it for the merry-go-round!) Your remaining tennis hope would be that your opponents were nice enough to lose to you. If you have other options, the net zone is no place for lobbing.

In this example, keep in mind that we are working through our shots from the net back to the entrance. Your second shot, if you are to stay on your three-shot schedule, has to be a transition shot that will enable you to enter the net zone. Using a lob to transition to the net zone is not a particularly good approach, since most replies to lobs are either return lobs or overheads. (Facing the latter, the net zone is about the last place to be.) If your opponents lob your lob back, you and your partner need to be on the service line to hit an overhead. It would be foolish to position yourselves in the net zone and hope they lob short when you know they're aiming over your head. Keep this in mind: LOBS DO NOT ENABLE FULL TRANSITION TO THE NET ZONE.

It seems reasonable to conclude that the entrance shot (serve or return-of-serve) makes the most effective use of the offensive lob. Ruling out lobbing as a serve, lobbing as a return of serve can be very effective when you find that your crosscourt return is not producing the desired results.

Lobbing The Return Of Serve

When you lob the return, clear the net player's head, without aiming for the baseline. You don't need a winner here, this is only your entrance shot. You still have two more shots (transition and net) to reach a "tactical 10." When you're sure the lob has cleared, move forward and take a court position as aggressive as you feel the situation warrants.

Most entrance lobs are returned as lobs. If you feel that is the case here, you and your partner should position yourselves on the service line. The opponent's intention is to clear you, and that is what you don't want. But, always give your opponent credit for being able to hit his target and position yourselves accordingly. If you luck out and his lob is short, you can always move forward. (Diagram #38)

When you feel your lob will be returned as a groundstroke, assume they'll be successful. Take positions at neutral net depth; this will make it more difficult for them to hit low and restrict your power weapon.

What Happens Next?

At this point you're looking to use your weapons in the net zone. If you're able to play your next shot from the net zone, it means the lob became your transition shot. Go straight to one of your "net" weapons. Since the player you lobbed has had to switch to the other side of his court, the most vulnerable spot on the opponents' court is his present alley. This should be your target because, if he positions himself at the net, he'll have little reaction time. And, if he moves back to the baseline, he opens up the angle. In either case, use your weapons to finish the point and remain on schedule. (Diagrams #39 and #40)

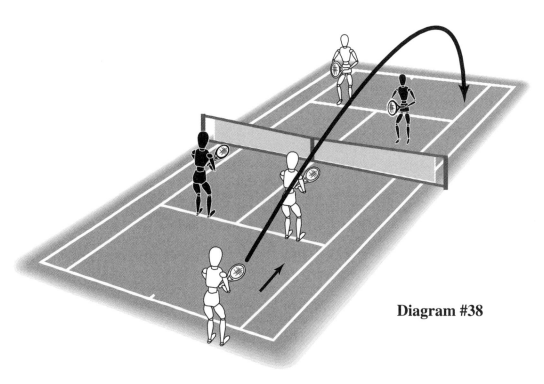

Diagram #38

Follow your lob in and take a position on the service line.
This enables you to handle a lob in return.

If, on the other hand, your opponents lob well enough to keep you in the transition zone and you don't feel your overhead is strong enough to win the point from there, hit a "transition" overhead. Accept the fact that you and your partner will have to hit one shot more than anticipated. (If you try to end the point with an overhead that won't do the job, you are trying to end the point with an inferior weapon and this will cost you consistency.) So, hit the transition overhead toward the deeper player, and wait patiently for an opportunity to move forward into the net zone where you're confident you can finish the job.

Handling Lobs From The Opponents

No matter how aware you are that your court position affects your opponents' shot selections, you'll get lobbed until they find it counter productive. Therefore, let's go over what to do when your team is the recipient of a lob.

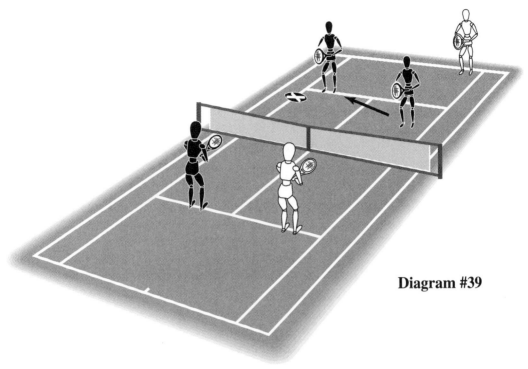

Diagram #39

After the server's partner switches, target
the alley of his new position to end the point.

Three situations can exist when your team gets lobbed: (1) you're happy they lobbed, because it's short; (2) you're in a little trouble but you can still get an overhead on it; or (3) you're in big trouble, since the lob cleared your head and forced one of you back to handle it post-bounce. Let's learn how to handle these three situations.

Handling Lobs From Your Net Zone

If the lob can be handled in the net zone, verbally communicate your coverage intentions as early as possible. The partner with the best overhead covers the middle.

Pick a target when you're handling the lob (or any other shot for that matter). In the present instance, choose an angle or the alley of the player with the least reaction time. If both players retreat to the baseline to buy reaction time, use the angle as mentioned earlier and shown in the diagrams.

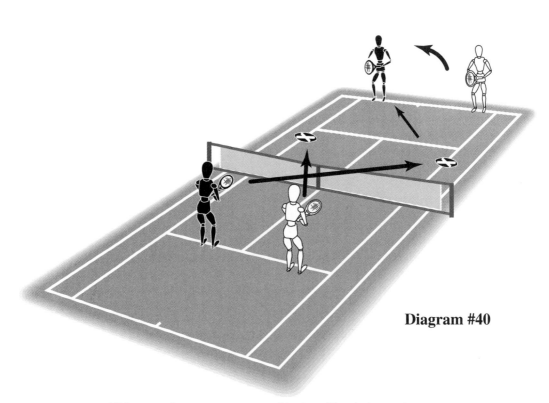

Diagram #40

If the server's partner senses trouble, he will switch to a deeper position to add to his reaction time. Both angles are now open.

Handling Lobs From Your Transition Zone

Some players can put away an overhead from the transition zone and some cannot. If you're comfortable taking this shot, follow the same rules you'd follow in the net zone (angles off the court preferably against the player with the least reaction time). If taking a particular lob feels too challenging to both of you, simply hit a more conservative overhead to the deeper player and wait for a shorter lob. Be patient. To retain the advantage of your court position, take the lob in the air. Remember, if they're dug in at the baseline throwing up lobs, they're not trying to beat you. They're hoping you'll be frustrated by their tactics and lose to them. But there's nothing nicer than competing against opponents who aren't trying to beat you. Thank them for their lack of aggression. BE CONSISTENT AND MOVE THEM INTO THE OPENINGS. Moving them will eventually result in a net-zone overhead opportunity. If you move them into the middle with the transitional overhead, your angles will still be available when you're ready to end the point. (Diagram #41)

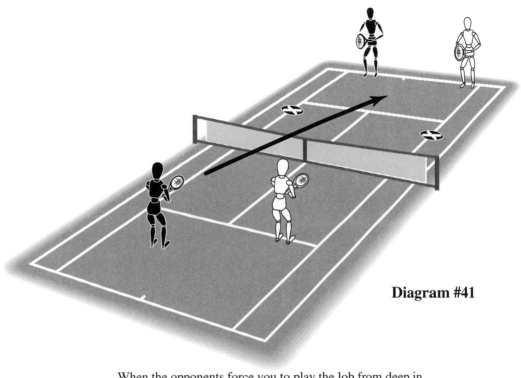

Diagram #41

When the opponents force you to play the lob from deep in
the court, be steady by playing a conservative overhead down the
middle. Hit the angle when they hit a shorter lob.

Handling A Lob Over Your Partner's Head

The most challenging lobs are those you have to handle after they bounce. Let's assume one of your opponents has hit a nice lob off your serve. The ball is successfully over your partner and he can't get it. When you move behind your partner to cover it for him, you vacate your own side of the court. To avoid double-coverage your partner needs to switch and play the side you were on, freeing you to handle the lob.

If you intend to *beat* your opponents, keep in mind that your team is hitting the second shot of a three shot schedule. To stay on schedule, you must transition behind this ball into the net zone (or at least have net zone representation by your partner). If this is not possible, the opponents have forced you into a situation where you may not have any offensive weapons available for five or six hits into the rally, if you ever have.

As you move to take the lob, check your opponents' court positions. Between the time they lob and before the ball bounces a second time on your side, you'll have about four seconds. This is a large chunk of time, don't waste it. Use it to choose your target and to decide how aggressive your return can be. (Diagram #42)

Diagram #42

Once the receiver lobs, you and your partner have about
four seconds to orchestrate a switch and emerge in control.

The opponents are hoping you'll decide to lob back so they can crush the overhead into your partner's alley. To avoid this, hit the ball low and down the line on the same side it came from. This will permit your partner to retain a net position because the opponents have no power weapon to encourage him to vacate. After you hit the ball, move toward the net where your weapons are located. (Remember your in-position closure, as the ball is moving away from your team.) If you choose to remain at the baseline and hit additional shots from the entrance zone, your chances of winning are slim. In fact, if your opponents are well schooled, you don't have a very good chance of recovering from a lob over your partner. (Diagram #43)

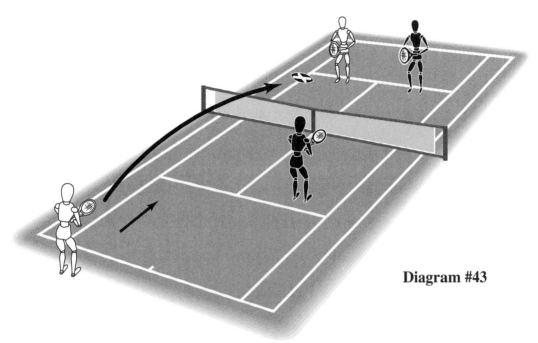

Diagram #43

When possible, return the opponent's lob with a
low shot down the line and move in. This provides the
best chance for retaining control of the net.

If the lob is too good for you to hit a low return, hit a return lob to the opponent with the worst overhead, or better yet, if the original lobber is still standing on the baseline admiring his handiwork, hit it to him. If you're in big trouble, buy time to get back into court position by throwing up a defensive lob. Your objective at this point is two-fold: reduce the availability of your opponents' weapons and insure that your partner can retain a presence near the net after he has switched sides.

Smart Switches

When your server leaves his side of the court to cover a lob that has beaten you, you must switch to take his vacated side or your team will have two players on one side of the court and none on the other. The shot your partner hits to return the lob will determine the exact position you take following the switch. To select the best spot, turn at an angle when you make the switch and glance at your partner and your opponents (as if you're having a conversation that includes all of them). The thought here is to gather as much information as you can to help you anticipate your partner's likely target and the shot he may hit toward it. (Diagram #44)

When switching, quickly move to the vacated court and position yourself
at an angle as if in conversation with all other players.
This is the most accurate way to anticipate your partner's target.

Diagram #44

For example, if you conclude that your partner either saw an opening down the receiver's alley, or he appeared to be hitting in that direction, you might switch to the spot near the net that's "in position" for a shot coming from the receiver's alley.

Note: To get the earliest possible start toward your in-position closure, watch your partner hit the ball. When you face forward and wait to clue off your opponents you are at the mercy of their anticipatory skills. In fact, if they are reactive rather than proactive, they won't even have anticipatory skills! Waiting gives you too little time to respond and complete your in-position closure, split-step and to-the-ball closure. Your objective here (as discussed in the anticipatory drill of Lesson 8) is to influence your opponent's shot selection through your court position. This means you have to have established it by the time your team's outgoing ball crosses the net. If you haven't done this, your opponents won't be able to see the position you've taken and cannot be influenced by it. (Diagram #45)

However, if your glance tells you that your partner can barely reach the lob, and you anticipate that he'll hit a defensive lob in return, you should take a stance far enough from the net to buy some time to defend against your opponents' overheads. Move back toward the baseline if your opponents have shown that they either hit their overheads at you or down the middle. Get as much reaction time as necessary. But remember, with each step you take backward to buy reaction time, you open yourself up to the angle.

As you know, this is a challenging situation. Not all lobs can be prevented but ... "an ounce of prevention is easily worth a pound of cure." You wouldn't be in this situation if you had anticipated the lob and returned it with an overhead, or if you had taken a deeper court position to discourage them from lobbing in the first place.

To Summarize

Offensive lobs are nice to have in your arsenal. But use them sparingly, since they don't permit you to thrive in the net zone. When playing a team that overuses the lob, patiently wait at the service line for an opportunity to use your weapons. A strong overhead to the alley of the player with the least reaction time is the best defense against the lob. When covering a lob over your partner, return low and down the line. When you've been lobbed, switch and try to retain the net.

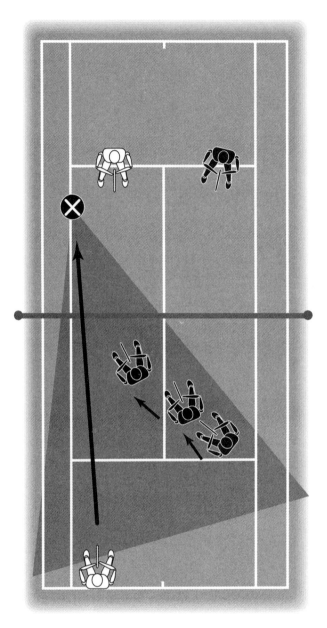

When your partner's shot supports your presence
in the net zone, quickly move into position. Then, aggressively
attempt to represent your team with its third shot.

Diagram #45

Point Control System Drill

For this drill you'll need four players. Split up into two teams and begin a point by serving to the deuce court. The receiver will practice his lob return-of-serve, then move forward. The server's "net man" poaches (pretending he anticipated a crosscourt return-of-serve) paying particular attention to moving toward the net strap. The server follows his serve in and split-steps, as though unaware that the return is to be a lob. Quickly, however, he sees and covers for the lob, returning the ball low and down the line. Meanwhile, his poacher has switched and taken the server's down-the-line target into account. The poacher then tries to get back into the point and retain the net advantage for his team. Play the point out and rotate players until everyone has played all positions in the deuce court, then do the same in the ad court.

Congratulations!

You've now completed the lesson on lobbing. You are now fully equipped to learn how to poach.

Lesson 12 - Taking What Isn't Given

How To Poach

Objective

Poaching is to the tennis player what a marketing division is to a business... the ability to go out and get what wouldn't come *to* you. This is one of the most powerful skills you can develop as a doubles player.

The Point Control System defines "poach" as taking a ball the opponents had intended your partner to hit. There are three types of poaches: (1) off your partner's serve to pick off the return (2) off your partner's return-of-serve, to pick off the server's transition shot, and (3) a mid-point poach; any poaching done after the previous opportunities. In this lesson you will learn how to poach off your partner's serve and off your partner's return-of-serve.

Why Poach?

The advantage of the poach over letting the ball pass through to your partner is primarily a matter of weaponry and the element of surprise. The poacher is closer to the net and therefore has more weapons available. When the poacher takes a ball intended for his deep partner, it permits the opponents less reaction time and catches them off guard. Poaching is part of ALL high-level doubles matches because it's a vital component in the process of winning a match.

Is Poaching Right For You?

Poaching is a skill and inclination some players develop and others don't. Poachers tend to be risk takers. They go for the gusto in life and are fairly aggressive personality types. They don't stand around waiting for the opponent to hit the ball *to* them. Instead, they go after it. They're always looking for opportunities to be pro-active even though they meet with occasional failure.

Why More Players Don't Poach

The primary reason more players don't poach is simply fear of failure. Visions of missed volleys, partner's disgusted looks, and getting passed down the alley are vividly portrayed in their minds. Perhaps this is because they have prohibitively high standards for what they would deem "success." Many players feel that to be a "successful" poacher they must hit every ball for a clean winner and NEVER get passed down the alley.

Some players even look to their partner for their sense of success. They need their partner to pat them on the back and say "Thanks.. you're the greatest! I know you get passed once in a while in the alley, but you're the best partner I've ever played with!" (When was the last time you poached and got that response from your partner?) If your standard for success is unreasonably high, you probably won't try to reach it.

"Successful" Poaching

Let's begin by creating a definition that will form a new set of beliefs for you as a "successful" poacher. Instead of making it difficult to attain success... let's make it easy. The Point Control System defines a "successful poach" as: an action that impairs the quality of the opponents' shot in any way, shape, or form.

With this definition in mind, you may now take credit ANY TIME your opponents hit a poor shot when you're in "poach mode." Their missed returns- wide, into the net or down the line- are counted in your favor. And, with each mistake your opponents make, your poaching self-esteem increases, until the history of your success significantly overshadows the times you are passed down the alley or miss a volley while helping cover the middle.

When To Poach

The Point Control System has no rules that spell out when to poach. Logic, however, should prevail. If your partner is serving (or receiving), and your team starts from the position that your goal is to inflict enough damage in the first three hits to win the point, only two hits remain in which you can be a factor.

Since your net position is more threatening than that of your transitioning partner, a savvy opponent will try to avoid you and hit to him. Should you let his shot go through to your partner, your team is now two hits into the point and you have yet to touch the ball. If your partner hits his transition shot, joins you at the net, then handles the next shot, you have been a non-participant in the point.

If you let this routine repeat itself point after point, why not take a seat on the sideline? You're not involved in the match and you're probably frustrated and not having much fun. Let me plant a seed: if you want to get into the match, look closely at the two hits that remain following your partner's entrance shot. After all, you're closer to the net than he is, so you have a better chance than he does to end the point. If you see an opportunity, go for it. Holding back does nothing for you, nor for your team.

Improvisational Poaching

The Point Control System uses improvisational poaching rather than the common practice of using signals. Here's why: signals can work when poaching is done off your partner's serve but cannot be used off his return-of-serve due to time constraints. Because of this limitation, I feel the best way to develop true poaching skills is by learning to read the evolving court situation and taking action on a moment's notice.

The Two Key Components

There are two key components to any poach: (1) you must anticipate the direction of the incoming shot you intend to poach, and (2) you must possess the mechanics to successfully reach and volley the ball to your chosen target. Although both apply equally to poaching off your partner's serve and poaching off his return, there are some distinctions to be made between the two. We will begin by learning how to poach off your partner's serve.

Anticipating The Incoming Service Return

A proficient receiver will have all three service returns in his repertoire: crosscourt, down-the-line and lob. Your poach will depend upon which option he selects. It's safe to assume he'll try to avoid you, so your job is to determine whether he plans to hit to your right, your left, or over your head.

His decision is primarily based on the weapons and court positions of the serving team. Therefore, to poach well you must first understand how your initial court position (your position prior to your partner's serve) affects the receiver's shot selection. For example, if you begin by taking a stance that is not neutral in the left/right dimension, you are inviting a down-the-line return. This is not conducive to poaching because you will not know whether the receiver will base his shot selection on the weapons available to your team and hit crosscourt , or on your court position, which invites the down-the-line. In this situation you'd be forced to cover the alley. (Diagram #46)

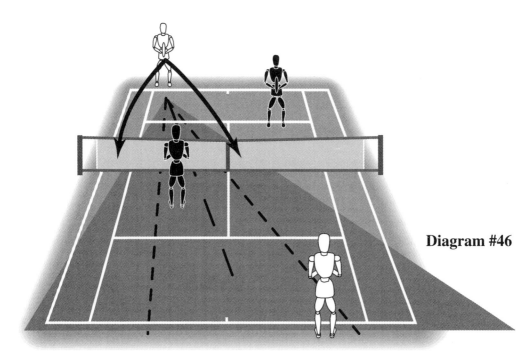

Diagram #46

Too aggressive a starting position will cause the
poacher to hesitate because the receiver will have good
cause to hit down the alley as well as crosscourt.

It is helpful to think of yourself as "poaching off the serve" because it helps you understand the role of the server in your success and failure. You and your server are working in conjunction to get you a volley in the net zone. This is accomplished through the quality of the serve and the server's ability to limit the receiver's options for return. For example, when your partner serves wide, the receiver may return down-the-line, lob, or crosscourt. But when your partner serves down the middle, the down-the-line becomes a less-likely choice because to successfully execute, the return must pass right in front of you. (Diagram #47)

Begin in the neutral left/right and front/rear position. Until your serving partner gets to the net zone the receiver will be encouraged to hit crosscourt to your deeper, less-weaponed partner. You should base your anticipation on your neutral court position and the conventional tendency for receivers to hit toward the player with the fewest

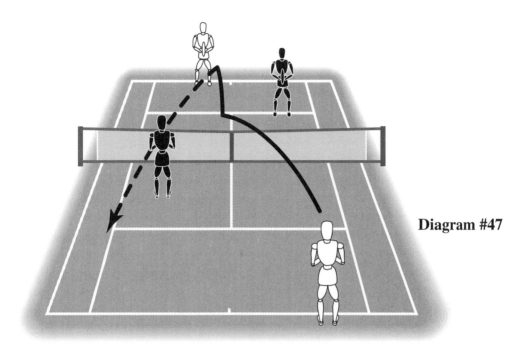

When your partner serves down the middle, the receiver
cannot access your alley without passing the ball right in
front of you. Therefore, this becomes an unlikely choice for return.

Diagram #47

weapons. This understanding, coupled with the serve down the middle should create enough probability for you to feel comfortable taking action (no matter how good you are there are no guarantees!).

Note: The better you are at receiving, the better poacher you can be. A player who overuses the down-the-line return, for example, will hesitate to leave his alley to poach. If your desire is to be a threatening poacher, limit your own use of the down-the-line service return.

Targets For The Poach

When you're cutting off a ball that your partner could handle, it's imperative that you inflict at least as much damage as he could. However, since you're in the net zone, it's expected you'll do MORE than he could (after all, isn't that why you poached?).

One of the keys to your success is choosing your target ahead of time. You have only fractions of a second to make decisions once your poach is underway.

Let's take a moment and explore the target options. There are three openings you could play to: (1) crosscourt to the alley, (2) down the middle, (3) back to the receiver's alley. However, not all openings will inflict the same tactical damage. Let's explore these options further so that you may decide which one is most appropriate. (Diagram #48)

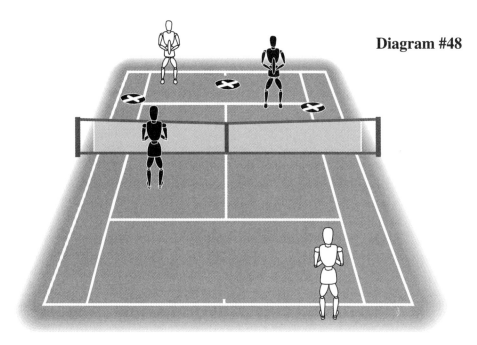

Diagram #48

The object is not to get the ball, it's to hit the ball to a target that's effective.
It will help to choose a target before beginning your poach motion.

Crosscourt To The Alley

This is by far the best choice in most situations and should be the target of choice for your poaches. You can do tremendous damage with your angle and reaction-time weapons when you choose to hit into the crosscourt alley. This is not only the easiest way to win the point, it carries insurance: if you don't hit a winner at first, you can stay in the point and go for it again because you'll already be in-position to reach the reply. (Diagram #49)

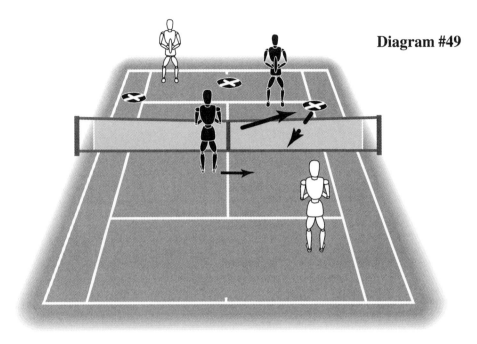

Diagram #49

The best target for your poach is the alley of the opposing
net player. This makes the best use of the angle and reaction time
weapons and allows the poacher to move again to the right to
handle a reply (should there be one).

Down-The-Middle

Down-the-middle is the second most productive target for your poach. At times you may have to forgo your angle weapon and, of necessity, hit to the middle. In this instance, your reaction-time weapon is also compromised, since the middle opening is shared by the deeper opponent who has more reaction time than the net man.

Back To The Alley

Usually, intercepting and hitting the ball to the opening in the receiver's alley is a poor choice. But with enough power and angle it MAY work if the receiver is still in the middle of his court. However, I strongly recommend you bypass this option because your chosen opening is now behind you. Hit a winner or your team will be scrambling to recover. (Diagram #50)

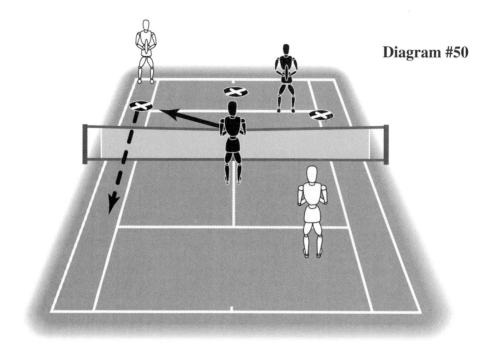

Diagram #50

Volleying back to the receiver's alley is NOT RECOMMENDED.
If you must, be certain to hit a winner or you'll face the down-the-line reply.

The Mechanics Of The Poach

Now that you've anticipated the incoming ball and chosen a target, it's time to help you reach that ball and do major tactical damage to your opponents without harming your own team.

From your initial neutral starting position in the left/right and front/rear dimensions, watch the receiver. Take a large step toward him with your alley-side foot while the serve is headed for the receiver (remember: in-position closure is always done when the ball is moving away from your team). (Diagram #51)

The challenge is to know exactly *when* the serve is on its way. To get this answer, watch the receiver (this is one of the few instances when you shouldn't watch your partner hit). If he steps forward to begin his return as your partner serves, he's telling you he's a hitter and you can start to time your forward closure. However, if there is no forward step, no intensity, just a blank stare (very common among less-skilled

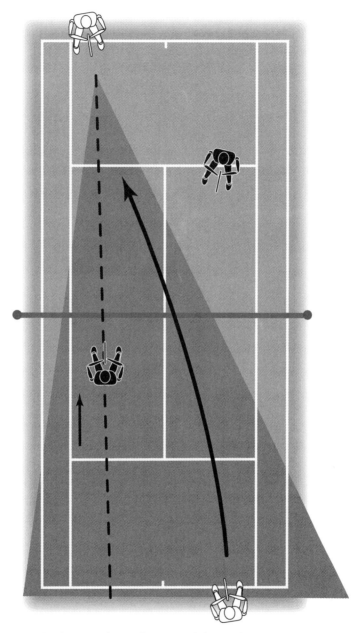

As the serve is moving toward the receiver, take one
large step forward with your alley-side foot.
Be sure to stay on the line of bisection.

Diagram #51

receivers), judging the timing for your forward closure is more challenging. In this case, listen for the sound of your server striking the ball to initiate your one step of in-position closure. When you step with your outside foot, you'll have a push-off point for your subsequent movement toward the center of the court.

Commitment

If you poach before the receiver has committed himself, you risk his change of mind and a hit behind you. But, take heart. There are two signs of commitment and you only need one to begin the to-the-ball phase of your poach. The order in which the signs appear depend upon the opponent and the situation, but either of them will signal that your opponent is committed and it's safe for you to move. "Safe" means that he cannot change his target; it does not necessarily mean that you correctly anticipated what his target was.

Forward Racket Motion

Forward racket motion is one sign the receiver (or any hitter) is committed to his chosen target. Don't mistake the backswing for the forward swing and you'll be fine. Watch the receiver and pick up on his timing. The longer his backswing, the greater time between his commitment and the moment he actually strikes the ball.

Eyes Off You

When the receiver takes his eyes off you, he's also signaling his commitment. No longer able to see you, he's basing his shot selection on your court position when he last looked at you. This frees you to poach. A skilled server knows this and will deliberately try to create this situation for his poacher by serving the ball down the middle or wide. Both these serves place the ball someplace other than between the receiver and the poacher which make the poacher disappear from sight more quickly as the receiver focuses on the ball.

Drifting During The Poaching Window

Once you sense commitment, push off with your alley-side foot and take two lateral steps toward the net strap, while still facing your opponent. This should feel like a drifting split-step done at an angle toward the net strap. Keep your shoulders square to the receiver as you drift. Ideally, (like a quarterback leads a receiver) you want the ball leading you toward your crosscourt target. When you run, or turn your shoulders, it makes it difficult to handle balls that don't show up exactly between you and your target. (Diagram #52)

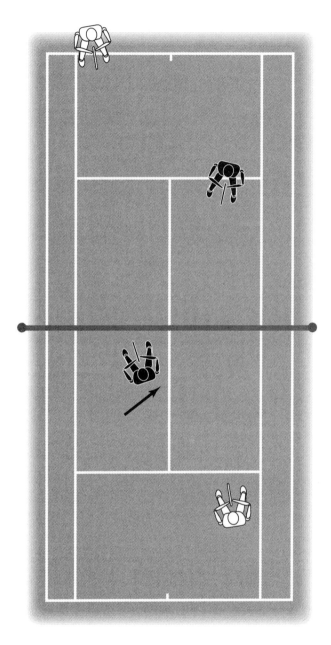

Once the receiver's eyes come off you or his racket begins forward motion, push off with your alley side foot and drift toward the net strap.

Diagram #52

Note: The primary difference between a poach and a regular volley is the leave timing of the "to-the-ball drift." Regular volleys are reactive in that you wait for your opponent to hit the ball, you see where it's going and then move to it (once you're sure of its location). Poaching is proactive. The drift begins in the millisecond between the receiver's commitment signal and the instant he strikes the ball.

Net Strap Is A Key Distinction

For several reasons it's very important that you drift toward the net strap when you poach. First, it lets you get to the ball before it drops below the top of the net. Once it does get lower than the net, much of the power advantage of your poaching is lost and you aren't much better off than your server in handling the ball. Second, by drifting toward the net strap you angle toward the path of the ball and cut it off with fewer steps. Third, if you have to abort your poach, the server will still have time to pick up the ball and keep it in play. And last, if you truly move into the corner formed by the center line and the net, you won't be crossing the center line. Crossing the center line often induces a switch from your partner and creates avoidable confusion. (More on that in a moment.)

As noted before, when you poach a ball your partner is perfectly capable of handling, it's imperative that you inflict AT LEAST as much damage as he could. Think of the net and the center line as forming a corner. Move into this corner to intercept the ball. Done properly, you're close enough to the net strap to touch it upon completion of your poach. (Diagram #53)

Making The Volley

Ease out of your drift when you have zeroed in on the receiver's return. It's ideal if you can keep the ball between you and your target without over-running it (you'll feel like the receiver of a perfectly thrown football pass). Once you see the ball and can determine its distance from you, make the crossover step with your front foot, go into your normal volley motion and use your chosen weapons to end the point.

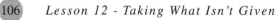

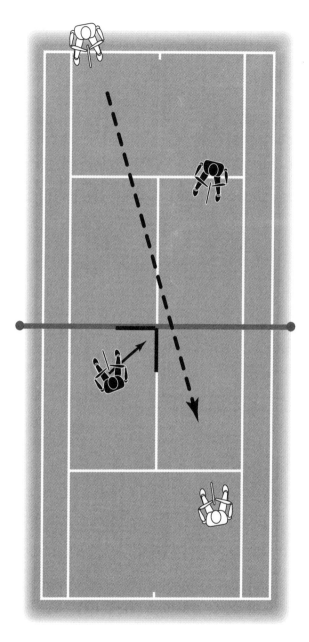

Move diagonally into the corner formed by the net and the center line. This will ensure that you get close to the net and take the shortest route to the incoming ball.

Diagram #53

Poaching Off Your Partner's Return Of Serve

Most of the same principles of poaching off your partner's serve apply to poaching off his return. However, there are several key differences you will find helpful.

Achieving "Success"

There is virtually NO DOWNSIDE to failing when poaching off your partner's return because you're not expected to win the game, the server is. If you can view this as a "no lose" situation, you will poach more frequently.

For example, your partner is returning serve and you feel he has set the stage for a good poach opportunity by returning low to the server's feet. You make your move but hit the poach into the net. Failure... right? Wrong! Momentary failure is often a matter of perception.

Let me explain. You didn't NEED to win that point, the server did. He's the one expected to hold serve. You made an aggressive attempt for a point you were not expected to win anyway. In doing so, you sent a message to the server that puts him under tremendous pressure. Each time you poach, you force the "poachee" into a situation where he must perform well or risk losing the point. When you continue the pressure throughout the whole match (even though you meet with occasional failure) you condition the poachee to feel pressure.

When it's six-all in the third set, and he misses an easy volley at deuce because he thought you would challenge him by poaching, you'll realize those past failures were a vital part of your victory.

The Receiver Sets Your Stage

The role of your receiver is to set you up for a poach. To accomplish this he needs to keep his return low and get it past the server's net player. Success will restrict the transitioning server's power weapon thereby allowing you more to-the-ball closure time (vital to poaching). In addition, your partner should aim his return as close to the center of the opponents' court as the server's partner will allow (taking into account his starting court position and poaching tendencies). The idea is to get the ball far enough away from the server's partner that he can't reach it, but not so far that the server can hit a transition shot down the line. (Diagram #54)

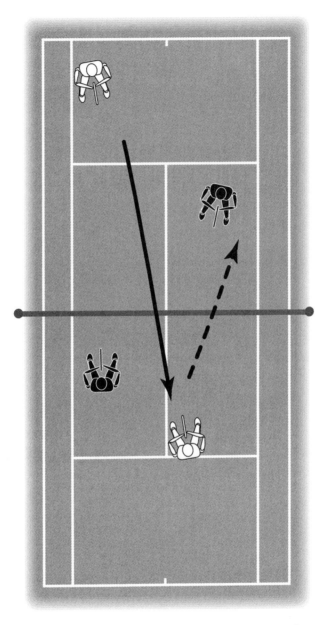

A return that exploits the middle makes it difficult for
the transitioning server to hit your alley.

Diagram #54

Mechanics Of The Poach

Begin on the service line in front/rear dimension and in the middle of your service box in the left/right dimension. From this central starting point you can make a relevant in-position closure regardless of your partner's return target.

Your body should be facing the server's net player because he is the first significant obstacle to your poach. From this position, you can watch the serve move toward your partner with only a minor head turn. Once the serve is on the way, follow its flight with your eyes and WATCH YOUR PARTNER HIT THE BALL. This will give you an early indication regarding the quality (speed and height) and destination of his return. Without watching your partner hit the ball, you will not have enough accurate information about the characteristics of his return to make a timely in-position closure. (Diagram #55)

Remain on the service line while your partner hits his return. As you know, this is too far from the net to be a serious threat (you're barely in the net zone). When your partner's return is headed for the server's feet you will do your in-position closure to the 1/3 mark. The time to do this begins with your partner's contact and ends when his return reaches the server. However, wait for your partner's return to get safely past the server's partner BEFORE you begin your in-position closure. Failure to do this will result in shortening your own reaction time if the server's partner decides to poach. (Diagram #56)

Once the return-of-serve is safely past the server's partner, take one step forward with your outside foot, watch for commitment (eyes off you or forward racket motion), and drift out for the ball with shoulders square to the server. Step into the volley and aim it to the crosscourt alley or down the middle. Using these targets will decrease, although not fully eliminate, your need to switch after your poaches. (Diagram #57)

Switching

Switching is one of the most critical aspects of poaching, and one of the most misunderstood. When your team is required to switch court sides, it is vulnerable to passing shots while this is taking place. So, SWITCH AS SELDOM AS POSSIBLE, while poaching as often as you see fit. If you move toward the net strap as you poach, and hit at an angle in the direction you're moving, you can avoid the need to switch. Also, this least complicated of the poaches not only avoids the switch – it avoids the confusion of the "I" formation.

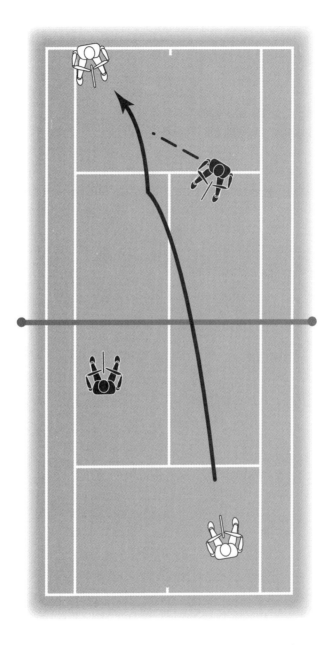

If you watch your partner hit, you won't be caught
off guard by the quality or destination of his return.

Diagram #55

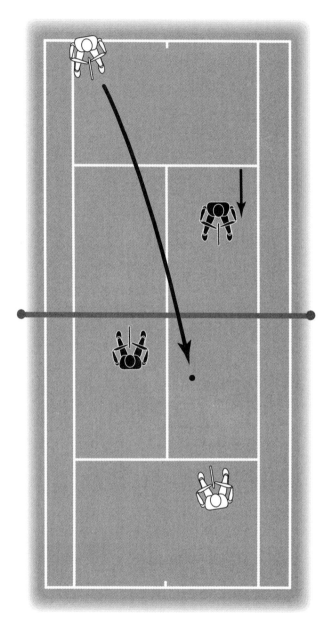

Wait for the return to pass the server's partner
BEFORE you start your in-position closure.

Diagram #56

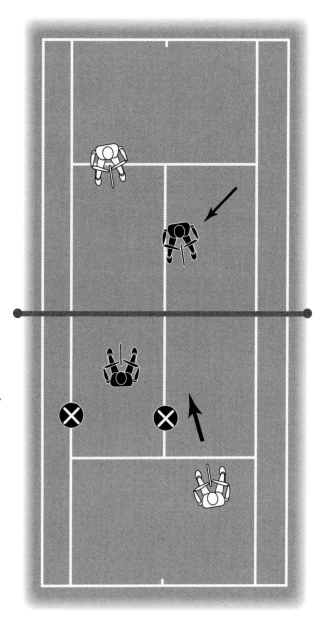

Wait for a sign of commitment and drift out for the ball.
Choose a target that makes the best use of your angle
and reaction-time weapons.

Diagram #57

The deep person is the one with the problem in the "I" formation. He's behind his partner and can't decide whether to go left or right. This is what creates switching confusion. The deep player, in this instance, is the server during his transition.

To minimize vulnerability, the server needs to enter the net zone on the same side of his poacher as he sees the ball. Ideally, this is the same side as when the point began and no switch is induced by the poach. (Diagram #58)

However, if the poacher volleys the ball down the middle or back to the receiver, it's possible the server will now see the ball on the opposite side of the poacher. This altered view of the ball's relationship to the poacher induces the switch and the server takes a net position on the half of the court vacated by the poacher. The additional time required to accomplish this creates vulnerability. (Diagram #59)

As a poacher, you have the responsibility of organizing your team to handle a reply to your poach, should there be one. Always consider that your poach may be returned, and remember you're the one who decides on which side of you your partner will see the ball. When you need to switch, do so without hesitation. If you linger around in the middle of the court, your puzzled partner will probably join you.

To Summarize

When poaching off the serve, use your initial court position to influence the receiver as you desire. Anticipate the incoming return-of-serve, step forward as the receiver becomes a hitter, drift toward the net strap on commitment and volley in the direction you're moving and stop to avoid switching courts. Remember to take credit anytime the receiver struggles.

When poaching off the return, remember to wait for the return to pass the server's net player before you do your in-position closure. Watch for commitment and volley in the direction you're moving.

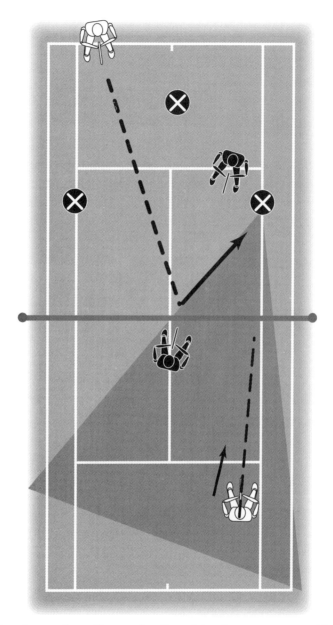

When the poacher volleys to the alley of the closer opponent and holds his position at the net strap, no switch is induced because the server sees the ball on the same side of his poacher as when the point began.

Diagram #58

When the server sees the ball on the opposite
side of his poacher, a switch is required.

Diagram #59

Point Control System Drill

You'll need three players for this drill, but four is even better. You have a server, a server's partner, and a receiver (and, if available, a receiver's partner). Take customary court positions and begin a point by serving to the deuce court. The server is to work on his serve; the net man on his poaching; the receiver on his returns.

The receiver, without trying to outguess the poacher, should hit everything crosscourt. He should concentrate on a target in the server's court and try not to be distracted by the poacher's actions.

The server's partner is to practice poaching. Work on getting the correct timing for the forward step (with the alley-side foot). Wait for commitment from the receiver, drift toward the net strap and volley toward the alley of the receiver's partner. He should practice getting to the net strap, then STOPPING after the poach. When done properly, a switch will not be required and the poacher will be close enough to touch the net strap.

Servers are to transition to the net on the balls that aren't poached. When the ball is poached, use the time during your partner's volley to get your court position at the net in position to handle a reply from the alley of the receiver's partner. Servers should not plant themselves in the transition zone and wait, assuming their partner's volley will put the ball away.

After an agreed-upon number of run-throughs with the first server, rotate court positions until everyone has practiced each of the (3 or 4) positions while still serving to the deuce court. When everyone has had practice in all positions, duplicate the drill in the ad court.

Note: The person receiving serve can help the poacher by telling him (afterwards) if he is moving too early. But, even if the poacher does leave early, DO NOT hit down his alley. Remember, this is a training exercise. Give the poacher a chance to develop confidence in a friendly, nurturing environment.

Congratulations!

You've now completed the final lesson in *Unlimited Doubles !!*. Please move on to the conclusion.

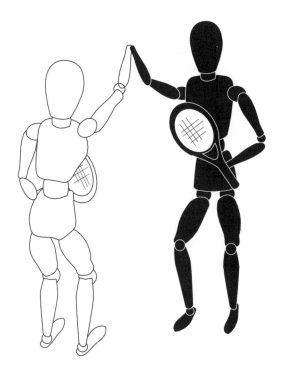

Conclusion

Tennis is endlessly fascinating to me because it involves, in almost equal parts, a mastery of technique as well as of one's own inner demons. Technique without self-awareness and self-control won't win a tough match. A player needs to control and overcome his own emotions and doubts as much as he needs to overcome his opponent's technique. He must believe he can win a match, and he must believe this at the most critical times in the match in order to prevail. Helping my students overcome their doubts about themselves and play to their physical limits is the most satisfying aspect of teaching tennis, to me. Virtually all players have the potential to play beyond their current level; they just need someone to show them the way. I hope I've done that for you in this book.

The lessons in *Unlimited Doubles !!* have been constructed to provide a systematic learning sequence for players who really want to improve their games. Reader comments are more than welcome, and can be directed to my website or mailed to Point Control Technologies at the address listed below.

Improvements to current lessons, as well as new teaching ideas will be available at my website: www.unlimiteddoubles.com. Stop by and register for the Unlimited Doubles Club- the only club dedicated to doubles players. Registration entitles you to receive free lessons each month and has many other benefits. I invite you to visit this site for further learning.

Enjoy your challenges, and good luck until we meet again.

Point Control Technologies
P.O. Box 819
Corte Madera, CA 94976
(800) 631-0673
www.unlimiteddoubles.com

About The Author

Steve Tourdo began playing tennis at age ten and gave his first lesson at sixteen when he agreed to teach a local businessman.

Success as a junior player landed him a tennis scholarship at the University of Nevada. After college, Steve gained world rankings in both singles and doubles on the professional circuit.

Now a popular tennis professional in Marin County California, Steve has twenty-three years teaching experience and a large following of recreational players who are his ongoing doubles students. His doubles groups focus on blending fluid movement with tactical prowess to win matches.

Steve organizes and coaches numerous men's and women's USTA teams ranging from 3.0 NTRP. to 5.0 NTRP. He is as dedicated to his students as they are to him.

An avid student himself, Steve's interests include martial arts, yoga, piano and homeopathy. To relax he's likely to go hang gliding or motorcycling and is already at work on two new videos and the sequel to this book.

Notes

Notes

Notes

Notes

Notes

Notes

Notes

Notes